Vietnam: Anatomy o

C000244153

Vietnam has experienced profound political and economic changes since the war. In *Vietnam: Anatomy of a Peace*, Gabriel Kolko looks at the economic program the Communist Party has embarked upon since 1986 and outlines the transition to nascent capitalism. He also explores reform's impact in demoralizing the party's members and the people.

Based on extensive research and first-hand experience, *Vietnam* is a vivid portrait of Vietnam today and the profound dilemmas it is confronting. Market reforms are producing serious social and economic difficulties in Vietnam; peasants are losing their land, inequality is creating a class society, and the industrial workers are amongst the most exploited in the world. In the light of these problems, Gabriel Kolko outlines how the Communists are failing to cope with the contradictions between daily realities and their original idealistic aims.

Gabriel Kolko argues that Communist efforts to merge a socialist with a market strategy have only optimized the worst aspects of each. The Communists have lost control over developments since 1986. After successfully confronting the United States in war, the Communists are now close to losing the socialist cause for which they fought.

Gabriel Kolko is Distinguished Research Professor Emeritus, York University, Toronto, and author of ten books, including *Anatomy of a War*.

Vietnam: Anatomy of a Peace

Gabriel Kolko

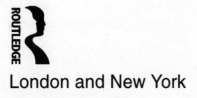

London and New York

First published 1997
by Routledge
11 New Fetter Lane, London EC4P 4EE

Simultaneously published in the USA and Canada
by Routledge
29 West 35th Street, New York, NY 10001

© 1997 Gabriel Kolko

Typeset in Palatino by
Ponting–Green Publishing Services, Chesham,
Buckinghamshire
Printed and bound in Great Britain by
T.J. International Ltd, Padstow, Cornwall

British Library Cataloguing in Publication Data
A catalogue record for this book is available from the
British Library

Library of Congress Cataloguing in Publication Data
A catalogue record for this book has been requested

ISBN   0–415–15989–x (hbk)
ISBN   0–415–15990–3 (pbk)

To Joyce, for all the reasons

To all those with whom I worked and shared a common cause, and who made this book both possible and necessary – once again

To Ho Chi Minh and those Vietnamese who earned and deserved far, far better

Contents

Acknowledgements

When I published my history of the Vietnam War, *Anatomy of a War*, in 1986, I acknowledged the great inspiration and assistance I had received over twenty years from an informal network of antiwar activists throughout the world who selflessly exchanged vast quantities of documents and information. They lived in the Philippines, Japan, Great Britain, France, Sweden, the Netherlands, and North America. This group's tremendous resources and skills were one way its participants could all express their profound political and moral convictions; their knowledge was a weapon against the war. Whatever differences on politics existed among us, all shared a deep commitment to peace. Without them I could not have written my book on the war in the way that I did, and to a crucial degree it was a common effort.

I made it clear then, as I do now, that I alone assume sole responsibility for everything I have written on Vietnam. Absolutely nothing I have said can or should be attributed, even indirectly, to anyone I have known over the past thirty years. This is especially true for the countless Vietnamese I have met since 1967, some of whom became good friends. Indeed, whenever I criticized Vietnam's actions to them, not once, without any exceptions whatsoever, did any agree with me; rather they either disagreed with me politely or usually listened patiently and never indicated approval of my opinions. We shared a deep respect for each other's convictions and motives, and nothing would satisfy me more than if that relationship were to continue in the future. Indeed, those who showed the greatest kindness to me also disputed my ideas the most.

Several of those I thanked in my book on the war have died, and others will unquestionably dislike my account of postwar

Vietnam. But new friends joined the informal circle with whom I have continued to collaborate. Their shared commitment to common ideals and to basic human values has been a great inspiration and encouragement to me. These values guided our common action during the war, and it has been a real satisfaction that many of us have continued to maintain them during the peace. I mention no names in this acknowledgement, but these friends all know who they are. It is to them that I renew the dedication I wrote in my book on the war.

Most important of all, my wife, Joyce, shared in every moment of this long chapter of our life together. Her insights and support were of inestimable value to me, and a large part of our sustained contact with Vietnam and Vietnamese was due to her prodigious efforts in every conceivable domain. This collaboration has been marvelously rewarding, and there is no way that anyone who has received so much from their life companion can ever express it adequately.

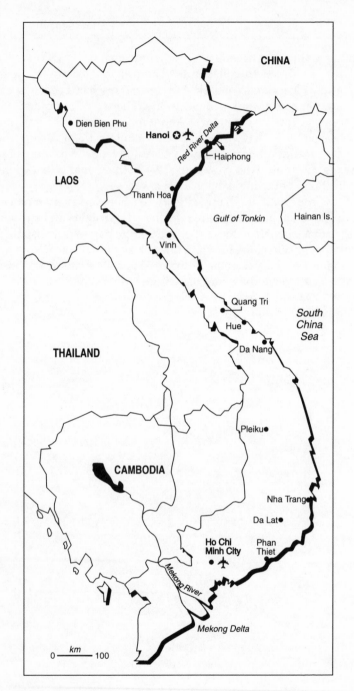

Map of Vietnam

Introduction
The legacy of war

The Vietnam War was the twentieth century's longest international conflict. In a world that has endured unimaginable protracted violence and suffering in vast areas, the Vietnam War was among the most devastating on people's lives. To grasp the enormous magnitude of this epic tragedy defies both words and imagination.

All wars profoundly transmute social and human realities, and it is only with this pervasive truth in mind that we can begin to comprehend the whole course of Vietnam's history, not only over the thirty years of the war but, above all, after it ended in 1975. There is a direct continuity between the war's overwhelming heritage and the two decades that followed it. We cannot understand the anatomy of the peace unless we fully appreciate the war's incalculable physical, human, and psychological damage, how its legacies defined the Communist party's structure and ideology, and left Vietnam destroyed and burdened.

It is a consummate irony – and tragedy – that many of Vietnam's Communist leaders, after a war that involved monumental sacrifices, within a decade of its end forgot their own history. They, of all people, could least afford to do so. For memory is not only an absolute precondition for fathoming the human condition and history's lessons, but above all for confronting today's challenges.

Although we are obliged to employ statistics to measure the war's impact, numbers can never capture the tears, anxieties, and repeated losses that the Vietnamese people suffered. Such experiences mock all efforts to plumb or describe them, and all wars must, however great our sensibilities, resist our attempts to comprehend them. Only those who have experienced or witnessed them can begin to sense their searing realities. Monumental human and social tragedies cannot be computed, and whenever we rely on statistics – nearly all of which are, at the very best, finite approximations – we also confess our inability to grasp realities that are far more profound and elusive. There are never census takers in wars in which civilians become principal targets; the victims are unable to keep records, and the perpetrators do not wish to do so. Crimes against humanity – and Vietnam was one of all too many in this century – are often virtually invisible.

Confessing that our addiction to figures reflects our inherent limits, the following are some of the most relevant: the United States and its allies exploded fifteen million tons of munitions during 1964–72, twice the amount used in all of Europe and Asia during World War Two. It sprayed defoliants, which cause cancer, birth defects, and other illness, on a fifth of South Vietnam's jungles, over a third of its mangrove forests, as well as on rice crops. About seven million South Vietnamese, comprising over half the peasants and one-third the entire population, became refugees and were forced into camps and cities, permanently for many, where degradation, vice, and penury brutally assaulted their traditional culture. Almost all of North Vietnam's industry, bridges, and transport systems were destroyed. Assessments of wounded and dead differ greatly, but in a nation of eighteen million in 1970, as many as 1,350,000 South Vietnamese civilians were wounded, with death for between a fifth and a third of this number. Over two million North Vietnamese soldiers and civilians were killed – altogether, about three million people died.

The Vietnam War's social and human effects, its incalculable consequences, and the profound moral and, ultimately, political obligations they imposed on the Communist party did not disappear when it was victorious in April 1975. Even if its leaders have forgotten this fundamental responsibility to an extent which, in hindsight, is as astonishing as it was unexpected, we cannot – and must not. For only then can we comprehend fully the anatomy of Vietnam's peace, and many of the crucial reasons why the Communists are well along the road to losing the victory for which millions suffered and perished.

*

The Communist party's major triumphs since its creation in 1930 were often the result of upheavals that began wholly independently of it but which at critical moments allowed, even compelled, it to enter vacuums that others were incapable of filling. In a crucial sense, the entire course of Vietnam's modern history has been the result of convulsions, the 1944–5 famine which killed about two million people and the Japanese defeat in 1945 being the most significant, to which the infinitesimally small number of Communists could, at best, only respond. But however accidental and improbable the triumphant Vietnamese Revolution of August 1945 appears at first sight, in reality it was no more unpredictable than the world war on which it was symbiotic, or many other modern revolutions. All wars have inevitable grave consequences, and a great potential for revolutionary upheavals is but one of them, increasing in likelihood the longer a conflict's social and economic effects traumatize the people engulfed in them. The major political changes in this century, whether from the Left or Right, would almost certainly not have occurred had there been sustained peace, and it is war rather than aspiring revolutionaries that has initiated the majority of those drastic changes our world has experienced. The principal challenge radicals confront is not to create a revolution, for by themselves they are utterly incapable of doing so, but what to do with success once it is achieved. Here too leftists largely fail, thereby neutralizing all they have attained or, even worse yet, leaving cynicism and disillusion in their wake.

Although Vietnam's Communist leaders were never wholly in charge, and perceived their role in ways that often bore scant relationship to the profound changes occurring around them, they possessed a sufficient sense of the times and their possibilities for them to seize and consolidate power. While they lacked the prescience and ideological insight they always insisted justified giving a handful of men the legitimacy to control absolute authority, they obviously nonetheless made many more correct than fatal decisions. They often failed to anticipate imminent major changes because their analytic equipment for doing so was much too schematic and deductive, but they were geniuses at exploiting the great historic opportunities that arose.

The fundamental dilemma facing all revolutionaries is that their talent to seize power is quite unrelated to the skills essential for administering and holding it. Each demands very different, and ultimately conflicting, aptitudes; the former benefits from speed and the absence at crucial moments of an inhibiting accountability to a mass constituency. Their very autonomy and the lack of control on their consummate pretensions to wisdom, and the absence of a formal obligation as well as of a real desire to win popular legitimacy, makes all authoritarian parties inherently dysfunctional vehicles for creating societies that attain their original social objectives. That they have failed to do so anywhere in the world in this century should have been much less of a surprise in the case of the Communist nations than it has been. Vietnam aspires to be the sole exception to this rule, and whether or not it can succeed is a vital question I seek to answer.

The Communist party's fundamental problem from its origins down to the present time is that the vast space and lack of communications, inherent in any comparable Third World nation, always made it extremely difficult for it to impose its tightly centralized and disciplined ideals on Vietnam's complex social and physical realities. The Communists' troubles in coping with such conditions, as well as their organizational theory, always caused them to fear localized upheavals and mass movements. Beginning with the spontaneous peasant uprising in central Vietnam in 1930–1 and the revolts in the southern Mekong Delta in 1940, the party's leaders attempted to impose their control over all activities carried on in its name. But if applying an elitist strategy in such a decentralized environment remained a continuous challenge to them, more daunting yet was devising ways of commanding a huge mass membership that was supposed to be highly indoctrinated and disciplined. The result was frequent failures and repeated crises, beginning with poor-peasant land reform campaigns after 1953, which seriously weakened the Communists in the north and made it impossible to reconcile their united front policy with radical mass movements that largely escaped the leaders' mastery. Several years later, the remnants of the party in the south forced the Politburo – the handful of men who run the party – to confront the huge challenge of reunifying the nation well before it wished to, and a southern poor-peasant land reform line was implemented despite its orders.

In effect, the party's chiefs repeatedly had to concede to mass pressures in the hope of guiding and controlling them, for they needed the people, whose strength and enormous sacrifices alone had carried it to victory in 1945, 1954, and thereafter. More important, the Politburo in Hanoi was frequently unable to dictate what was actually being done in remote areas with which it usually had scant, if any, contact. The absolute necessity of decentralizing the war organization throughout the provinces after 1963 only accelerated the growing disparity between a Politburo, with its centralizing pretensions and theory, and realities. This gap between Communism's elitist organizational theory and actuality was the irreversible logic of vast space and wartime conditions. As we shall see, it created the context for today's growing rivalry for authority between the Politburo and many of the local party organizations, each with its own jurisdiction and ambitions.

The party's leaders were generally very able tacticians, but ultimately the only valid justification for their hierarchical organization, in terms of public legitimacy, was the emergency that war itself created and their capacity to cope with it successfully. Although their authoritarian command structure during the war had crucial assets, in practice their orders were often interpreted liberally, or sometimes ignored entirely. But once the conflict ended in 1975, the party required either consummately brilliant and able men at the top, which neither Vietnam nor any other nation in history has ever possessed permanently, or the creation of an open, flexible organization far better able to adjust to the peacetime challenges it faced.

The Politburo never believed that mass mobilization would eventually require genuine popular participation and democracy both within the party itself and the nation at large. It possessed a supremely successful wartime organizational theory, which reflected conditions of hard struggle and sacrifice, but nothing adapted for victory and peace. No one even contemplated the possibility that a consummately elitist doctrine that triumphed in one environment might be irrelevant, even highly counterproductive, in a radically different one.

Most Communist leaders were essentially able administrative problem-solvers drawn principally, as in China, from the intelligentsia and the wealthier classes, but they were overwhelmingly men who mastered a simple litany of phrases and had an astonishingly superficial theoretical and analytic capacity. As one senior official once confided to me, when he joined the Revolution in 1945 neither he nor his peers knew anything of formal Marxist theory, implying he had scarcely improved since then, but that their children had studied it in school and they knew far more about it! Of the virtually hundreds of Vietnamese Communists I met after 1967, at every level from the grass roots to Politburo members, none incorporated Marxist or Leninist doctrines into their thinking in any meaningful way and, more important, very few even attempted to do so. One must read through vast quantities of writing to find analyses that even pretend to be truly informed by historical or dialectical materialism. As the party over time became institutionalized, all too many Vietnamese Communists were no different from people in successful parties everywhere: their overriding concern was power.

By the early 1970s, many of the key party leaders were political only in the most superficial sense, and although their cause was on the verge of victory, they were astonishingly incapable of sensing the mood and potential of the period. Party chairman Le Duan's advocacy of the scientific and technological revolution, and the army's comparable plans for the military, opened the door for nonideological administrators to move to the fore. After the 1973 Paris agreement they expected a long period of no-war and no-peace, confusing the party at a decisive point when it required a far more acute insight into the nature of the war. As I detailed in my *Anatomy of a War*, published in 1986, the Politburo's assessments reflected this increasingly technocratic, remarkably apolitical interpretation. This deepening intellectual myopia reflected a profound malaise that after 1975 only became more acute.

The balance of forces in any war, but especially one of this nature, far transcends the conventional equation of military power. But the Communist leaders increasingly believed the war's outcome depended on material resources. They grossly underestimated those crucial social, economic, and psychological factors that determine victory or defeat in war. They had very few, if any, experts who could competently analyze such matters, but from this perspective it was obvious by mid-1974 that the war could not last much longer. The Saigon regime's political and economic crisis was already very acute. When I visited Hanoi at the end of 1973 and attempted to discuss South Vietnam's economy with Tran Phuong, then head of the North Vietnamese social science organization and later vice premier in charge of the entire economy, I was amazed not only by his inability to define the problem of social dynamics in the south but by his self-satisfied – and, it turned out later, disastrous – ignorance of quite elementary facts about its economy.[1] The party was more preoccupied with the economic reconstruction of the north, for which it seriously expected U.S. aid! In late 1973, when I visited South Vietnam, National Liberation Front officials who asked me about the war's possible duration responded with frank skepticism to my prognostication – already too conservative – that it would end within two years; most of them believed that ten years or even longer was much more likely. I have no doubt whatsoever about Communist calculations, for when in February 1975 I met the future foreign minister in Geneva and told him I believed the war would very soon be over, only three months later in Hanoi he confessed that he had thought I was "crazy."

Nonetheless, the errors the Communists made during the war cannot detract from their overriding success in attaining victory, for whatever reasons – whether the foibles of others and success by default or their own wisdom, but especially the enormous courage and privations of their people. The leaders who were triumphant under the most daunting conditions in wartime have been infinitely less able in coping with the peace, thereby casting a grave shadow over the nation's epic struggle. For the irony of Vietnam today is that those who gave and suffered the most, and were promised the greatest benefits, are gaining the least. Their rulers are abandoning them to the inherently precarious future of an economy which increasingly resembles the system the United States supported during the war. For the majority of Vietnam's peasants, veterans, and genuine idealists, their struggle is becoming a vain sacrifice.

The Communists won the war well before they were prepared to confront the Saigon regime's overwhelming problems. Total victory came as a complete surprise, and the patient habits the party leaders had cultivated over a thirty-year struggle severely dulled their comprehension of realities. Throughout that time, notwithstanding their sacrifices and frequently brilliant sense of short-range tactics, they succeeded to a very great extent because of the immense errors and corruption of the Japanese, French, Americans, and Saigonese, who fought their wars in brutal and politically counterproductive ways. It was also this stupidity that gave the Communists much of their nationalist legitimacy and access to the masses, whose monumental suffering and devotion proved sufficient to attain victory. But essential qualities the Communists had honed to near perfection before 1972 were largely irrelevant to their peacetime challenges, for now they could no longer survive on their enemies' blunders. The vast responsibilities for managing the south, with the prodigious problems of reconstructing the nation materially, socially, and psychologically, and repairing the infinite varieties of damage that had been inflicted on the people, now fell entirely upon them.

This book begins where my *Anatomy of a War* ended.

DEALING WITH THE PEACE

My fundamental assumption is that the thirty-year Vietnam War profoundly defined the peace that followed, and only such a perspective allows one fully to understand its profound legacies – including, above all else, the nation's expectations and the party's responsibilities. This legacy, of course, was obviously economic: the war's physical damage and urgent reconstruction needs, decades of neglected development, and infinite material problems. Foreign observers tend to reduce every nation's basic problems to economics, because to judge them in all their inordinately complex dimensions defies numbers and requires far greater knowledge and sensibility. But in Vietnam's case such simplifications are impossible, for its single most important challenge after the war was to rebuild the lives of millions of civilians and soldiers who had suffered and sacrificed without limit. They expected – to say nothing of deserved – that their needs and problems would receive the highest priority, and the party both explicitly promised and morally obligated itself to use the peace to fulfill its historic compact with the masses. Economic criteria alone cannot be employed to judge any society's success, least of all one that claims to be socialist; Vietnam's social, political, and human conditions are therefore the subject of the larger part of this book. The only just and rational gauge must be the lot of the people.

As disillusion, fatigue, and cynicism have become pervasive, the most fundamental challenges the Communist party has faced since 1975 have been social, political, and even psychological. The economy is both a cause and an effect of these trends, and it is impossible to disentangle exact causal relationships. As everywhere, but especially in Vietnam, a nation's true condition cannot be judged primarily in economic terms. Least of all can it be understood with the amoral criteria that official economists in ostensibly socialist and capitalist societies alike all now employ.

The Communist party since 1985 has articulated a new rationale for its economic reforms, and the only thing it has in common with its earlier economic ideas is the same dogmatic certitude with which it has justified two diametrically opposing positions. This stance is the inevitable consequence of its credo that the party cannot, by definition, be wrong. After nearly a half-century of asserting that socialism differs from capitalism in crucial ways, and proving it by applying its premises to pursue the war successfully, the majority of its rulers were converted to the notion, which became the nearly hegemonic economic ideology throughout the world only after the inception of the Reagan–Thatcher era, that all economies under all circumstances must surrender to the same ostensibly immutable objective laws of the market, whoever is nominally in power. This market is universally justified with fictionalized history.[2] It requires nations to alter drastically their standards for individual and group conduct, and in Vietnam's case to reconcile the selflessness it demands from party members with the acquisitive behavior which is the precondition of a market economy. Its efforts to do so have produced fundamental moral ambiguities and conflicts, affecting profoundly both the economy and the party. Its leaders deplore this glaring contradiction publicly but increasingly tolerate it in fact. Chapter 1 deals with the origins of this striking tension between a market theory and socialist values.

The party's economic doctrine has produced results we can measure generally in terms of growth rates, trade, and the usual economic indicators. Far more elusive, but potentially the most significant and enduring development of all, is the extensive de facto privatization of state industry and commerce that is already far advanced. Starting from premises identical to both the Soviet Union and China, the three nations share very strong similarities. Chapter 2 surveys the major economic changes that have occurred since 1986.

The way in which the party has confronted its growing internal contradictions is of decisive importance. The Politburo is nominally entirely in command of an organization spread throughout the 1,500-kilometer-long nation, but the reality in many towns and provinces is often very different. For practical purposes no one has challenged its authority directly but its power is slowly but irresistibly being eroded from under it because the provincial party organizations are escaping its grasp. Even more dangerous to it, innumerable party members, abandoning themselves to the new economic policy and their own ambitions, are openly pursuing their personal goals; many simply ignore their ostensible obligations, and they regard membership as a means of advancing their careers or, far worse, corrupt goals. The party's morale has plummeted, creating a crisis that has profoundly shaped the nation's social and cultural life and, above all, determined who is gaining (or losing) the most from economic reform. Party membership is a crucial prerequisite for entrepreneurial success. This far-reaching transformation of the party, and the Politburo's growing inability to control it, is the focus of Chapter 3.

The most important changes in Vietnam since 1975 have occurred in the countryside, where over three-quarters of the people live. When the Communists totally abandoned the public land ownership system that had existed for thirty years, the impact was enormous. It has produced mounting social and economic instability and conflicts among the peasantry to an extent few outside Vietnam appreciate. The rural social system is being transformed fundamentally, and this traumatic process has created a large and growing number of discontented, marginalized peasants. Thousands of protests, demonstrations, and even violent confrontations have occurred since 1988. The peasants made the Revolution possible, but only because the French created a land system that impoverished the already poor rural masses. The very party that the peasants sacrificed so much to bring to power is increasingly dispossessing a significant fraction of them. At the very least, this policy can delegitimize the Communists' pretensions completely, but should rural social and economic relations continue to deteriorate, a potential mass base for opposition to the party in the future will be created. Chapter 4 outlines this crucial problem and challenge.

Chapter 5 surveys how social services, such as education, health, and housing, are being redistributed, and the contours of the class society that is emerging. The most immediate consequence of this trend is reflected in rice and food consumption. Vietnam today has more poverty than any large Southeast Asian nation, and a significant fraction of the people are undernourished; it still lacks sufficient food to feed the entire population adequately, but since 1989 it has become the world's third-largest exporter of rice. While rural conditions and high unemployment explain some of the reasons for poverty, the small but growing urban working class is the lowest paid in Asia. It is also becoming more and more alienated, and hundreds of illegal strikes have occurred – and the number continues to rise. The Vietnamese Communist party is increasingly facing neglected peasants and discontented workers.

The Communist party has confronted these disturbing, anomalous developments while profoundly disunited, and a very significant minority within it deplores this retreat from the original principles and motives that alone produced its victory in war. This division is already profound, growing, and very public. For a party that says it demands absolute unity, it has far less of an internal consensus on fundamental goals than many western parties that label themselves democratic. Political dissent outside the party is entirely constrained, but there are no inhibitions whatsoever on people living as ostentatiously bourgeois a lifestyle as they can afford. Indeed, they are encouraged to get rich. Facing all these obvious contradictions has created a grave, essentially irreversible crisis within the Communist party, one that is exacerbated by the fact that the new privileged economic class – those who can afford to live like the bourgeoisie – is to a large extent emerging out of the party itself. Widespread nepotism and corruption, which no "market" theory attempts to explain, is a major consequence of attempting to put it into practice. In Chapter 6 I discuss the enormous political and moral trap the party has worked itself into and the split that has resulted.

Vietnam: Anatomy of a Peace focuses especially on the period from the mid-1980s through the June 1996 eighth party congress, which was intended to be a new departure for the disunited party but only ended in further dividing it and producing a stalemate that reflects the irreconcilable moral and intellectual crisis from which it is unable to extricate itself. The years between the end of the war in April 1975 and the beginning of the Cambodian war at the end of 1978 was a troubled, improvised transition, and that war, with the great constraints it imposed, lingered until 1989. In a crucial sense, true peace only then came to Vietnam.

An anatomy of the peace must describe what the Communist party has done with the great opportunities for which it struggled heroically over thirty years, and how it evolved politically as the nation was transformed socially and economically. But when the history of Vietnam is written a century from now, the war and the peace that followed will be treated as a single, indivisible experience – one monumental challenge confronting the Communists, who after defeating many enemies had then to master themselves in order truly to achieve their ostensible goals. It is also likely to confirm that exploiting peace, and justifying a people's immense sacrifices, requires even greater wisdom than attaining military victory.

HOW AND WHY *VIETNAM: ANATOMY OF A PEACE*

This book is the necessary, even obligatory, sequel to my account of the Vietnam War, *Anatomy of a War*, which I published in 1986. It surveyed the Communist party's victory in war, and *Vietnam: Anatomy of a Peace* describes its imminent defeat in peace. And like its predecessor, it is the result of an odyssey that began over thirty years ago and permitted me to observe closely one of this century's great historic events. Without such a profound experience this book could never have been written, nor would it have been required. It is certainly not a *mea culpa*.

I offered my book on the war without apologies. I stated then that I was from the inception totally opposed to all American involvement in Vietnam – and everywhere else for that matter – and favored autonomous socialist economic development in the Third World, including Vietnam. I was an anti-interventionist long before the United States became directly engaged in Vietnam, and that remains my opinion today. I wrote then that I have always deplored the hegemonic pretensions of the Soviet Union, China, the U.S., and all nations that aspire to dominate others. I have been a socialist my entire life but I have always believed that neither Marxist-Leninism nor social democracy have offered, either in theory or practice, ideal or feasible alternatives to attaining a rational society based on social justice and equity.

Modern socialism has comprised specific parties that arose in response to distinctive historical situations, and the labels they adopted scarcely describe their real behavior or theory, much less what they have in common with other parties utilizing the same name. That socialism cannot or may never be attained does not mitigate capitalism's inherent inability to serve as the rational institutional standard for a just society or peaceful world, or lessen the need for a fundamental alternative embodying socialism's original objectives and inspiration to resolve many of the world's enormous problems. I consider this predicament in my Epilogue.

In the Epilogue I also describe in greater detail why I justifiably opposed what was an unconscionable American attack on the entire Vietnamese people, their culture as well as their lives. Whatever has occurred since then has in no way altered my opinion on the absolute necessity and justice of having done so. I spent a very considerable part of my life after 1964 resisting the war, and I always favored allowing the Communists to retain the mandate which the majority of the Vietnamese people gave them after 1945, one they very well may have lost had French and then American imperialism not brutally assaulted their nation and renewed the party's authority. Foreign attempts to reverse Vietnamese self-determination loosened the awesome dragons of war and destruction, at an incalculable cost to every nation involved, in what became a sustained, terrible crime against humanity.

I always expected the Vietnamese Communists to do far better in power than the Russians or Chinese, and in certain important regards they have done so. By 1975 I also anticipated some of the postwar problems, problems which I thought would be serious, not the least because the concentration of so much power in the party Politburo's hands removed any check on both its abuse and, what proved to be even far more dangerous, its ignorance. But I scarcely suspected it would employ its victory to create a "market" economy, which is merely a euphemism for capitalism. Like everyone else, without exception, I lacked the imagination essential for comprehending this often surrealist period of history we are now living through.

In *Anatomy of a War* I wrote that there was no tension between my partisanship and commitment to attaining as objective an assessment of reality as was feasible. Indeed, I asserted that the very possibility of a serious independent Left ever emerging was conditional wholly on optimum clarity and candor as well as hope, and we could no longer afford the illusions of both social democracy and Leninism if we were ever to reverse the injustice and transcend the problems that capitalism has imposed on much of the world over the past century. My book neither could nor should be taken seriously unless it had been completely independent and as honestly researched and reasoned as possible. The credibility of the radical, humanist ideal in this age of profound cynicism and disenchantment is precisely in its uncompromising willingness and effort to explain reality in its totality, its complexity included, as objectively as possible. While many reviewers praised it, such candor in *Anatomy of a War* quite predictably upset those who favored the war or felt equivocal about what they justifiably interpreted as a friendly view of the Communists. It was by no means uncritical, for the Vietnamese translation excluded much that deprecated them, obvious points that traditional Cold Warriors had no ability to perceive.

Vietnam: Anatomy of a Peace reflects exactly this identical critical posture. Those who supported the war and now welcome Vietnam's conversion to the market – and, in essence, the ultimate American victory over socialism – are likely to deplore it also. This is precisely as it should be.

Ironically, my aggressive independence made the insights that have gone into my book on the war, and now the peace, both possible and necessary. It was with this total candor that I interacted with literally hundreds of Vietnamese after 1967, both in France and Vietnam, and witnessed some of the great dramas of the war. Between 1968 and 1975, I wrote three widely reviewed books and dozens of articles on diplomatic affairs and the war, all directly relevant to Vietnam, in which I always asserted strongly my independence of both the two Communist giants and the United States. The Vietnamese whom I met never had any illusions whatsoever regarding my opinions. My very first political encounter with a Vietnamese, in May 1967, was with a once very senior diplomat who sought to prevent my imminent public statement before the Bertrand Russell War Crimes Tribunal in Stockholm that the Russians and Chinese pressured the Vietnamese into signing the Geneva accords of 1954. We had a tense, direct argument, and to his frank surprise and dismay I remained obdurate. He reported to others that I was an anticommunist, but rather than discredit me, this only increased my credibility among some Vietnamese who justifiably resented their allies' past betrayal as well as the danger of their future treachery. When a reviewer in the *Moscow News* accused me in 1970 of anticommunism for my book on World War Two, a Vietnamese official gave me a copy. As a result of this frankness, I was never treated condescendingly like an innocent antiwar American, which would have instantly prevented future contact. In subsequent countless discussions with Vietnamese, I always told them what I believed they should know and never what they wished to hear. This usually involved bad news, and I published innumerable articles that cast open doubt on many of their optimistic private as well as crucial public assumptions, such as my very pessimistic prognosis for the 1973 Paris agreement, in which they naively had placed great hope. They often disagreed but they always listened attentively because I never asserted a position without documenting it carefully. I was continuously a gadfly, but I was right sufficiently often to be taken seriously. We learned a very great deal from each other, and this critical, absolutely honest relationship only increased our mutual respect and growing friendship.

After 1971, when I began to live in France for long periods, I had continuous, intensive, and deeply rewarding meetings with National Liberation Front and North Vietnamese personnel working in Europe. These frequent discussions occurred because I informed myself as much as possible about every aspect of the war. The Vietnamese I met were very careful and good listeners, and I did most of the talking; they were courteous and silent, but extremely attentive, when I warned them after 1971 of possible impending perfidy from the Chinese, Russians, and Americans. Many with whom I maintained contact over the years eventually assumed important responsibilities, in a number of cases becoming members of the party central committee or Politburo. Whatever it symbolized, my wife and I were invited to be the first Americans to visit South Vietnam after the Paris agreement.

My research concentrated especially on economic and social trends within South Vietnam and the acute political crises they were creating. American agencies produced virtually all of the information on South Vietnamese domestic affairs that existed, and I had far greater access to it than the Communists I knew, most of whom could not read English. Some topics were highly specialized, such as the offshore oil potential that surfaced about 1971, but the World Bank's quiet efforts to sustain the wobbling Saigon regime became my principal source of information on the condition of the economy and rural society. I wrote extensively on these topics, and much of what I learned over fifteen years went into my volume on the war. By chance, I therefore began to prepare intensively for this book twenty-five years ago. *Vietnam: Anatomy of a Peace* reflects this emphasis on objective economic and social developments and how they interact with political forces. I have approached the postwar period sensitive to many of the same problems and sources. Considered in isolation, these factors lack an adequate sense of dynamics and fail to grasp how societies actually evolve and change dramatically. The war marginalized and displaced a large proportion of the population. The peace is doing so also, much less traumatically but relentlessly nonetheless. At some point such combinations create their own momentum, and people and institutions increasingly transcend a government's control in various ways – some are small, others large, but the sense of community and social cohesion dissolves irresistibly.

From late 1973, when I first visited both North and South Vietnam, I emphasized the probability of such seemingly discrete elements combining to challenge the Thieu regime and weaken his army. I frequently cited the analogy of China during 1945–8, when the Communist armies were much smaller than the Nationalist forces until the final months of the war. Military victory followed from a sociopolitical collapse, and did not produce it. This thesis was greeted with open skepticism or silence, but in March 1975, when precisely this scenario began to unfold, my wife and I were urged to come to Hanoi immediately, and for five weeks we had intensive, sustained discussions with people at every level, up to the highest, on internal and international affairs. How to cope with the southern economy was a major topic. On several occasions my wife and I lectured, including on conditions in the south, to people who were even then being snatched from various departments to be sent there to create an administration. Some were very able in their vocation, but one senior diplomat of our acquaintance was taking a crash course on economics and he did not conceal how bewildered he was. He, and many hundreds like him, went south. I spent the final four days of the war in Hué and Danang in the south, and everyone I met was equally perplexed and uncertain. Much optimism was still left over from the war and the euphoria of victory, but there was no economic plan, nor even a rudimentary mastery of essential economic information.

Those Vietnamese who should have known far more failed to comprehend adequately what was most decisive to the war's outcome. They have shown much the same myopia and naive simplifications in coping with postwar challenges.

After April 1975 I lived in France part-time and remained in regular contact with economists and officials trying to adapt to the new conditions. In October 1976 my wife, Joyce, and I returned to Vietnam for seminars and discussions principally on economic topics, as well as for a close look at the south. During the summer of 1977 my wife gave a five-week course in Hanoi on the world economy, including discussions, that brought together about a hundred economic specialists from the party, universities, bank, and ministries, many of whom had never met each other before. This long exposure enabled me to gauge the state of economic knowledge in crucial places.

Medical problems prevented me from returning to Vietnam until 1981, and I also visited again in 1983 and 1987, when I was able to see and discuss trends in the society in general. During this last trip, when I firmly criticized the new economic policy, our disagreements were sharp, relations sometimes exceedingly uncomfortable. I was for the first time invited to the party's luxurious headquarters, which is housed in an elegant French-colonial building, and without the usual protocol or even normal courtesies, a spokesman coldly delivered an astonishing hour-long lecture on the virtues of "free enterprise." I could scarcely utter a word. The line was set, and bad news was not welcome. It was my last visit.

After then, I followed events closely in the daily U.S. Foreign Broadcast Information Service and other sources. Meanwhile, letters and occasional meetings with Vietnamese in Europe and the United States helped me to understand their thinking. All of our encounters were now informal, relaxed, and entirely frank. We disagreed about a very great deal, but by now we were good, often close, friends, who had shared many precious experiences. Friendship remains, and I earnestly hope this book will not change it. Indeed, for those Vietnamese who increasingly now share my concerns, after sincerely believing that the party's new program would prove successful, perhaps it will even strengthen our comradeship, because I very well may be raising fundamental issues they themselves will or can not. Best of all, if this proves to be the case, would be for my effort to gain new friends. In any event, no one will accuse me of changing the critical, uncompromising basis of what has been for three decades an immensely rewarding relationship, much less of forgetting the reasons that brought us together in the first place.

My Epilogue is a defense of what I and countless persons throughout the world, who shared many remarkable years together with courage and idealism, did together during the war. It also discusses the mandatory obligations we must now assume lest the Vietnam experience discourage those who are very likely in the future to be called upon to make great personal commitments and solidarize with people in a nation that is being subjected to some of the terrible inhumanities that were inflicted upon Vietnam.

The modern historical experience has been infinitely complex and enigmatic, full of enormous ironies and tragedies. Our most urgent task is to prevent cynicism and disenchantment that generates apathy in the face of injustice and oppression. But we cannot defend the obligation of resistance to them in the future unless we are completely honest about the past, however great the sensibilities of those who share or perpetuate illusions about it. Hence *Vietnam: Anatomy of a Peace*.

Chapter 1

The postwar economy and the origins of "market socialism"

When the war ended in 1975, Vietnam's leaders had no coherent plan for dealing with the southern economy, much less the skills and organization that the immense challenge demanded. But even had they prepared one, the problems of unifying the two regions would still have remained awesome, not the least because the southern economy after 1972 was already in a deep crisis. The thirty-year conflict had imposed monumental economic, social, and human costs on the people and the party. Whatever the advantages of one or another economic strategy, there was no conceivable way that recovery could be easy or painless.

Worse yet, the party's leaders failed to grasp that any general reconstruction program had to be effective not only in terms of economic growth rates but also in its ability to resolve the war's more intangible but crucial social and human challenges. Many no longer believed that those who gave and suffered the most during the protracted conflict had imposed binding obligations on them. Ironically, had the Communists conducted themselves during the war in the same unimaginative, empiricist manner they have displayed since 1986, reducing their grand strategy to gauging success in narrow accountancy measurements, they certainly would have lost it.

Leaders who had shown extraordinary creativity and sensitivity before 1975 began increasingly to absorb the mind-set of those they had defeated. Their elitist mode of operating frequently isolated them from the information and criticism essential to avoiding serious errors. Long used to commanding and being obeyed, they failed to comprehend that the masses – above all the poorer peasants – had willingly sacrificed to a significant extent because they had confidence that the nationalist and social causes were identical, and the latter was in their objective interests. This combination, and the promise that their immense devotion would be rewarded when peace came, gave the Communists the legitimacy that had created a remarkably high degree of national consensus during wartime – one they could not afford to lose. Without it, their problems would be even greater. Under no circumstance whatsoever could they allow the so-called winners to become the eventual losers. Ho Chi Minh had always warned that the party must never lose touch with the masses.

The triumphant party in war was unprepared for peace, both in the narrower organizational sense and – as it turned out – in its moral relationship to the people.

THE INHERITANCE OF WAR

Until 1975, the exigencies of the protracted war shaped Vietnam's economic and political structure decisively, and while the Leninist influence on it cannot be minimized, neither can its strong resemblance to capitalist war economies under comparable circumstances. The decision to fight a war is based on overriding political priorities that later have inevitable and enduring economic and social legacies. During wartime, victory is the only criterion for economic efficiency, and the Communists were supremely successful. But many of the leaders could not imagine that the economic and political methods appropriate to war might become counterproductive in peacetime, and there was no way anyone within the party could discuss this risk seriously.

To divorce Vietnam's economic development from war-induced causes, as International Monetary Fund (IMF), World Bank, and Establishment economists have persistently done, reflects capitalist economists' endemic ideological inability to view politics and economics as intrinsically related dimensions of one unified social reality. Most nations locked in wars will go to extraordinary lengths to win them, and subsidy-based economies and consciously induced distortions are the rule rather than the exception. Germany, Britain, and the United States, to mention but a few after 1914, repeatedly gave huge subsidies to expand industries, transport systems, and much else that was subsequently largely useless in peacetime economies. Few, if any, of Communist Vietnam's

economic policies from 1955 to 1975 differed in principle from
what states normally do during wars.

Vietnam's regionalization of the economy and transport was the
only rational course possible insofar as some production at low
levels of efficiency was superior to a centralized alternative that
theoretically was more productive but also offered American
bombers better targets. The cooperative and collective agricultural
system was a precondition for manpower mobilization, since it
provided security to soldiers' families and allowed for optimal
employment of women workers. That both might create major
problems after the war was unimportant. There was only one goal:
to win the war in the face of vastly superior military and economic
power. The Communists triumphed in what was certainly one of
the most unequal conflicts in human history, and they initially
interpreted this as a vindication of their economic and political
policies until then. On the other hand, they failed to perceive fully
that their French and American enemies' uncritical faith in material resources was proof that the complex nature of societies and
their problems made a fixation on power in the strict physical and
economic sense exceedingly dangerous. Until 1975 the Communists insisted that they had depended on ideological and broader
social factors that alone made them succeed over the long run.
Ironically, after 1986 they increasingly adapted many of the
assumptions and human priorities of those they had defeated,
priorities on which a consensus has prevailed throughout the
world since market theory attained unchallenged ascendancy in
the putative socialist nations.

From a purely political and military viewpoint, Vietnam's
economic structure was eminently rational and efficient, for it was
a decisive factor in producing victory. Astonishingly few, if any,
Vietnamese now assess the war's burdensome economic and
organizational legacies in this essential historical context, or their
integral relationship to current economic problems, just as they
ignore the social implications of their present economic course to
the party's chances of future survival. And this fact alone is a
reflection of the utter inadequacy of their superficial ideological
resources for dealing with the immensely complex environment
in which they live.

In a word, it was the unavoidable Communist decision up to
1975 to make those sacrifices essential to winning the war that
created the overall context for their economic experiences after

that date. While choices within that framework unquestionably produced quite distinct short-term results, the Vietnamese leaders' present misinterpretation and rejection of their past economic efforts perilously misjudge history and have primed them for more errors than the existing system is able to bear.

Whatever the Democratic Republic of Vietnam's (DRV) historic aid dependency, which unquestionably made its war economy far more viable, it was nonetheless much smaller than the south's reliance on U.S. support. Southern agriculture was not only structurally different in 1975, historically it had always been much more individualistic than the north's, and however great the local peasants' earlier political role, most refused to accept the co-operative systems that had succeeded fairly well in Annam in the center and Tonkin in the north. And while the DRV was in certain ways poorer than the south, it had a far superior social infra-structure in terms of health, education, and the like; the merger of the two zones immediately posed huge difficulties in this domain also. The Communists were totally unprepared for these gigantic challenges.

The dominant southern economic class has always been over-whelmingly Chinese. When Nguyen Van Thieu in 1966 seized power in Saigon, a small coterie of Chinese worked with him to play the leading role in exploiting South Vietnam corruptly. Wealthy Chinese began exporting large amounts of capital well before 1975, and when Saigon fell their personal connections in Southeast Asia allowed many to go into exile and prosper else-where. Given this elite's political as well as economic role, and the inherent fragility of the dependent, parasitic southern economy, there was no conceivable way that Vietnam's leaders could have left its power untouched. Apart from the consequences to morale as well as to their ideology, had the Communists avoided con-fronting them it is highly likely that the local Chinese would eventually have thwarted the creation of a socialist economy, and grave economic problems would have arisen in yet other forms. It was impossible, from an economic or political viewpoint, to merge the two regions painlessly. The situation after 1975 was ripe for a crisis – and it was one that involved Peking's traditional protective relationship to Southeast Asia's overseas Chinese.

It was at this very point that Vietnam's conflict with Cambodia after December 1978 altered fundamentally the entire context of reconstruction and gravely compounded the war's already immense burden. However justified the political and security reasons for its invasion of Cambodia in December 1978, economically it was a catastrophe, above all at this critical point, producing a world economic boycott that constrained economic development and consumed vast resources for another decade. Its short, extremely destructive war with China in 1979 imposed an additional huge drain, forcing it also to remain mobilized on its northern border. Vietnam's economy, to varying degrees, never became fully geared to peace until it evacuated Cambodia and the world boycott was lifted after 1989. In this context, the decisive origins of its economic problems were political, the consequences of having first fought the Americans to the utter limit and then becoming embroiled in the region. No conceivable economic strategy, whether socialist or capitalist, with or without a "market," could have caused genuine reconstruction. Indeed, it was certain that once real peace came then significant growth would occur also, whatever the policy. Politics, not a plan, was the principal constraint on the economy as well as impetus to its economic growth after 1988.

The party's leaders have refused to this day to acknowledge in any way this fundamental reality because it only would confirm the immense economic costs of their Cambodia strategy, one whose justification became weaker as the war lingered indefinitely and the government it installed in Phnom Penh became increasingly venal and even nationalist. Worse yet, many blamed their economic failure until then on their refusal to accept the putative "laws of the market." But attributing the price of their political error to an economic policy only compounded the party's serious analytic failures. From the very inception, its economic assumptions after 1978 largely ignored the vast political, social, and human charges inherent in both its wars with the U.S. and especially Cambodia, and it never comprehended that its economic policies had not only to produce growth but at the very same time weigh them against its more intangible but imperative social obligations to the people. This fundamental myopia distorted its priorities gravely, and it is likely to stand as the greatest single mistake that the Communists made after 1941.

OPTING FOR RENOVATION: *DOI MOI*

In certain ways, the data we have show that the economy in the decade after 1975 might have been much worse, and later official accounts of it exaggerated its failures to justify the new economic strategy. In 1977 the party began to take over the property of the mainly Chinese southern bourgeoisie, disrupting the non-agricultural as well as the rural economy and antagonizing China in the process. Apart from the Cambodian war's great impact on every aspect of production, and the doubling of the army to 1.5 million men, 1980 was a catastrophic year for agriculture; a series of typhoons destroyed at least 40 percent of the north's rice crop, and the war absorbed all resources that might have been used for essential imports of fertilizers and food. The disastrous conjunction of the war and weather forced the party to introduce or simply tolerate major revisions in the entire agricultural marketing system, with its pragmatic emphasis on increasing output in any way that succeeded. Ideology remained, but practice changed, and this was also true for large sections of industry. "The stomach is our principal concern," officials admitted.[1]

Between 1976 and 1980 Vietnam's agricultural policy had fortunately emphasized food other than rice, and by 1980 overall production had increased to 61 percent above that of 1976. Rice is by far the major staple, and the introduction of an extensive contract system after 1980 caused yields to increase steadily. Agricultural output grew a fifth from 1979 to 1982. Given the low base from which it began, this impressive record was far from brilliant. Much more significant, from 1981 to 1984 grain output increased 4 percent and paddy 6 percent annually, or 21 percent for all staples in 1981–5 – not very different than subsequent growth.

Industrial production, assuming that the official data are reasonably accurate, also grew 54 percent from 1981 through 1985. Considering the low quality of much of the output, these numbers are less impressive, but that is equally true of much of the growth since then. The economy had serious problems, but it was never as calamitous as Vietnam's promarket leaders subsequently described it, nor as bad as it might have been given the external circumstances. Most important, to repeat a crucial point, the party has kept silent regarding what was, in fact, the principal cause of the post-1977 economic crisis: Vietnam's protracted war with the

Pol Pot regime and then the brief but terribly costly conflict with China in 1979.[2]

Whatever the rhetoric, there was far more pragmatism than ideology guiding the economy, and many sections of the nation pursued their own, often quite different, economic strategies. In 1981, largely autonomous regional import and export companies were authorized, and there was, and always has been, far less central control over state enterprises than in China or the Soviet Union. Indeed, when the Politburo was unable to articulate solutions for problems during the early 1980s, it explicitly decided to "delegate powers to the regional and grassroots echelons," in reality reducing its own.[3] Some provinces even taxed goods coming from the others. A province-centered economy was the inevitable legacy of the war and the nation's vast length, and this is even more the case today.

Such independence made it possible for the party in Ho Chi Minh City, led by Nguyen Van Linh and Vo Van Kiet, to permit the local Chinese merchants after 1981 to reimpose their control over the regional economy, leading to its rapid growth. Linh was a key Politburo member and Kiet was also chairman of the crucial State Planning Commission; his assistant was Nguyen Xuan Oanh, whose unusual background and even more remarkable role warrants more detail here.

Nguyen Xuan Oanh probably has had the most varied and remarkable career of any single person in Vietnam since 1944, but in the last analysis the real source of his power was the party's inability to employ its socialist ideology to respond to the vast challenges facing it. During World War Two he collaborated with the Japanese and received his BA in economics in Japan in 1944, and an MA in 1947. He then worked for the U.S. Army in Japan and went on to earn a PhD at Harvard in 1954. After an un-distinguished career as an academic in the U.S. and a minor IMF functionary, he returned to Saigon in 1963, becoming vice premier in charge of the economy in 1964. As acting prime minister in February 1965 he gave the Saigon regime's endorsement of the American escalation of the brutal air war against the DRV. A coup soon removed him from office, and he spent the next years in Saigon preparing a plan for Vietnam's postwar economy which, as a U.S. Defense Department intelligence expert later described it, "was very similar" to that which he was later to convince Linh and Kiet to adapt.[4]

Linh and Kiet authorized Oanh to use local Chinese to create and supervise mixed trading companies, and these firms quickly became extremely profitable and allowed the city to prosper for two years in what the same Pentagon analyst described as "unfettered market capitalism."[5] The favored Chinese had close connections with the local party leaders, and in mid-1982 the Politburo in Hanoi learned about what was then considered scandalous, possibly corrupt, behavior. Linh was dismissed in disgrace from the Politburo because of his zeal, but his success in the south soon became decisive for the party's future. Kiet himself is both avaricious for power and result-oriented; doctrine for him is merely ideological baggage to which he gives obeisance but which scarcely influences his actions. He can cite Marxist rhetoric to justify his goals but he is no more a socialist than were Yeltsin and his cohorts. Linh, as subsequent events showed, is unquestionably very sincere but he has scant understanding of economics. He proved himself to be as impressionable to Kiet as Kiet was to Oanh. Oanh was certainly not wholly in charge, but his influence was crucial at a time when the party, paralyzed by its dogmatism, lacked constructive alternatives. Meanwhile, the IMF in its annual consultations, which Vietnam's membership in it required, was urging the same policies. Oanh was also a natural link with the IMF, for which he once worked. I will continue this astonishing story in the next chapter, after Linh and Kiet took charge of the national economy in 1985 and the IMF's role became decisive.[6]

Vietnam's leaders throughout the early 1980s were profoundly confused and disunited over how to cope with an increasingly diverse economy that they guided far less than many of them desired. It is a simplification to call it a centrally planned socialist economy, because while that was the ideal and a major part of the reality, it was also much more complex. In fact, central control has been far less of a goal than producing results, because over the long run, as in China, real power in the economy has been moving toward the provinces, and the Politburo became aware of the risks of this shift only well after it had embarked on them – or too late. In an effort to resolve its economic impasse, in June 1985 Linh and his allies were readmitted to the Politburo and central committee, and they initiated major steps to reduce subsidies to state enterprises and begin market-style reforms, called "socialist account-ing." Tran Phuong, whose abysmal ignorance of economic affairs had so impressed me when I met him in 1973, was made vice premier in charge of the entire economy. He was always, and still remains, a devotee of the market. It was under his supervision that Vietnam's most critical problem ceased to be growth and became inflation.

Retail prices between 1979 and 1985 rose consistently, nearly doubling in 1982 alone, destabilizing the economy seriously. In September 1985, Phuong and the reformers sought to reverse this pattern and organized a currency reform which produced a disastrous hyperinflation and far graver difficulties than at any time since 1979. Prices over the next year increased at least 700 percent and created a monumental crisis, and there was a disastrous decline in output of every sort. Phuong was fired in total disgrace but the damage had been done.

What had been a serious problem before 1985 now became a major emergency. The situation had been poor, but it was now far worse. The so-called reformers' first major innovation was cata-strophic, but they were able to retain control, and even consolidate power over the Politburo. Ironically, having produced a totally avoidable crisis, because of their sheer incompetence bolder action now became imperative, and the reformers were prepared to take far greater risks yet when Linh in May 1986 became the party's secretary-general. Six members of the Politburo were replaced, and since the opponents of the market line lacked constructive alternatives, they acceded to most of their plans; the reformers defined both the spirit and letter of "market" economic reforms for the next three years and, for practical purposes, their imple-mentation since then.

In the next chapter I describe the period of renovation, *doi moi*, after their accession to power.

The Politburo confronts the economy

The very political nature of the Politburo renders rational eco-nomic decision making inherently difficult, if not impossible, and since 1980 all of its economic policies have been vague and usually contradictory. As an elite of fifteen to twenty men seeking to retain absolute control over the party, the Politburo strives, above all, to maintain the internal cohesion within its own ranks which is the precondition of its putative mastery over the party and state. It places a greater priority on its own unity than on making difficult or coherent choices that might endanger its corporate identity and role. To maintain it requires compromises that repeatedly produce the lowest common denominator in economic policy, which invariably leads to indecision and an openly incongruous quality in many of its plans. But while it always describes its mutual toleration as unity, it has increasingly been in deep disagreement on many crucial issues. This inherent ambiguity in the funda-mental political structure has allowed many officials, both in the national and local governments, to define policies to suit their own interests. Ironically, by attempting to maintain its absolute polit-ical hegemony in this consensual fashion, the Politburo has created a degree of freedom of action in the lower party ranks that has produced a cacophony of often-conflicting policies. There are so many faults inherent in this system that Hanoi's economic and political control has been gravely challenged in practice.

The Politburo was able to sustain the pretense of its consensus until about 1994, when the mounting problems brought about by guiding the economy in this fashion began to generate increas-ingly irreconcilable differences among the top leaders. After that, the façade of unity began to crumble, resulting in an open split in 1996.

While the Politburo in 1986 unanimously refused to acknowledge publicly the decisive extent to which the Cambodian war and the world boycott it provoked were responsible for the economic crisis, it understood that it was imperative to extricate the nation from that quagmire. It took three years to do so. Given its extremely critical attitude toward the economy's successes until then, which ignored how, basically, socialist forms had won the war and remained potentially viable, by 1986 the majority of the Politburo concluded its principal problem had been its refusal to obey the universal "objective laws" that ostensibly guide eco-nomic affairs everywhere, whatever the context.[7] These putative inevitable forces allegedly necessitated much less state control over markets and prices, and significantly more independence for state industry and the rest of the economy. Since both Marxist and bourgeois theories assume that laws impersonally control all economic affairs, it was simple for the Politburo to use Marxist logic to reify a "market" economy once wholly identified with capitalism. Official ideologists instantly produced an imposingly obscure theoretical litany to justify the revelation that a "market" stage was really integral to the ultimate transition to socialism. This evocation of laws has only grown with time, but after decades of altering doctrine to justify its changing policies, many senior party members have become increasingly immune to all ideas – and cynical. Such doctrinal gyrations simply devalue all theory, good and bad, and the ensuing confusion increasingly has deprived the party of core principles, which at this point it needs more than ever.

Had the party defended resorting to the market as a purely tactical expedient and temporary measure, a pragmatic case might have been made for it, especially if it retained those existing institutions and policies that were still viable. Instead, it bestowed the same blind faith in the market it had once given to total central planning, and its new ideological concoction again locked it into the inexorable logic of history. In abandoning a very large part of the socially positive achievements of the past, it revealed not just a lack of deep socialist values but a total ignorance of economic history, a myopia reflecting the basic intellectual underdevelopment of those who pretended to be able to guide the nation. Putative economic laws simply do not explain how economies evolve in reality, and market theory has no conception of how the state and politics, or social power, invariably define economic development profoundly.[8]

In fact, the real reasons for the Politburo's discovery of "market laws" at this late stage in the party's ideological development were far from objective, and cast a profound shadow on both its sincerity and judgment. The principal factor was the Politburo's wholesale acceptance of the ideas and policies that Mikhail Gorbachev articulated during 1985–6, and which quickly led to the "spontaneous" privatization of Soviet industry and were instrumental in the collapse of communism.

In addition, however, by the mid-1980s many key party leaders serving as economic officials were practical problem solvers who were uncomfortable with doctrines of any sort. Their ability to get results, which was particularly strong among the leaders of the southern party who had honed this pragmatism to a high degree during the war, caused them to rise to the top. All Communist states after they are firmly institutionalized have produced talented administrators who are frequently socialists in name only. In the USSR such people readily abandoned ideology and abolished socialism, and their being in decisive positions was the logic of the system's leadership selection process. Their precise equivalents exist in Vietnam and China also. Cynicism among this element is rife. In 1981 a French-trained Vietnamese technocrat who worked for the United Nations and was very influential in Hanoi told me that Communist leaders could be converted to a market economy only if it were couched in ostensibly Marxist terms – and such a concoction soon became the official line.

Vo Van Kiet, who has been prime minister for most of the period since 1986, and his deputy Phan Van Khai have far more influence over functional economic and state administrative affairs than the army or exclusively party leaders, and any socialist rhetoric they employ – and they do so more and more sparingly – is a necessary afterthought. Most of the economic administrators under age fifty, and often much older, are technocrats in the strictly objective sense, frequently relatively able, nearly all very ambitious personally, and quite like their peers in capitalist societies. As was also the case in the Soviet Union, many are apolitical opportunists and often corrupt. Like the Soviet apparatchiks, they could easily and happily fit into an avowedly capitalist society.

Notwithstanding the party's evocation of arcane theory to the contrary, there has never been a truly indigenous basis for its new market ideology. Those who conceived it considered themselves administrators rather than theorists, and they chose to rely on its assumptions, above all regarding human behavior, to stimulate economic growth. The dilemma, as the IMF was soon to learn in China and Russia at the same time, was that many of these pragmatists were no more devoted sincerely to market doctrine than they were to socialism. Given the complexity of the problems they confronted, the question was whether aggregate economic growth alone could resolve them. Would the party's eclectic opportunism create an inherently unstable porridge of capitalist and Communist ideas, and in the end be truly practical? Indeed, no one contemplated that such a synthesis might maximize many of the worst aspects of both systems.

Chapter 2

Economic reform in theory and practice
The crisis of success

When Vietnam's leaders embarked on *doi moi* in 1985, they were profoundly confused and their highly abstract deductive ideas could not easily be translated into concrete action. Their first major innovation in September of that year, currency reform, only gravely aggravated an already critical economic situation. In the following February the Politburo made a private "self-criticism" but it issued a contradictory, abstract economic guideline which failed to offer meaningful guidance.[1] The leaders faced an impasse, for which their vague rhetoric offered no solution, which only encouraged them to take even more dangerous risks. Vietnam had very serious problems before 1985, but now they were much greater.

As the IMF later described the two years after reform began in mid-1985, "the reform effort ran into trouble almost immediately"; conditions, if anything, were substantially worse than during 1983–5.[2] Production fell sharply in agriculture in 1987, inflation in both 1987 and 1988 was over 300 percent and further impoverished workers and government employees, the distribution system worsened, and unemployment grew dramatically. There were widespread food shortages throughout most of 1988, bordering on famine in some northern provinces. At the end of 1987 the central committee released an unprecedentedly sharp attack blaming the Politburo for the failure. In March 1988 the state bank introduced a new currency and again botched it: food prices doubled within a few days, the value of the dong dropped by almost a half.[3] The Politburo and economy were both at an impasse, paralyzed; the basic problem was that neither side in Vietnam's leadership had a viable economic program to offer. But the reformers were in charge and utterly devoid of a coherent or practical strategy, for the "market" was no more relevant than orthodox central planning. Vietnam's rulers were treating the people with utter disdain, which is politically risky anywhere but especially where the state ideology defines a social criterion against which their actions could be measured.

THE IMF REFORMS SOCIALISM

It was in this total policy vacuum that the International Monetary Fund began to play what was to prove the decisive role in determining what the "dictatorship of the proletariat" has meant in reality since 1986.

When the Vietnam War ended, the victors retained the Saigon regime's membership in the organization, and this requires an annual consultation for all its members. IMF staff reports recommended the recipe it urges, without exception, for every nation: flexible pricing, fewer exchange controls, reduced subsidies, export promotion, private foreign investment, and market conditions – in effect, the abolition of a socialist planned economy. The invisible market would replace a plan! These proposals initially received very little attention, but Vietnam had debts of about a billion dollars to non-Communist nations that had to be serviced, and IMF loans were essential to making this possible. In mid-1982 it threatened to terminate them unless major structural reforms were introduced, and it specifically praised the policies that Linh and Kiet had introduced in Ho Chi Minh City – measures which had led to Linh's removal from the Politburo.[4] It remained on the sidelines, but its crucial leverage over Vietnam's debt always enabled it to gain an audience. Even more important, however, was that the party's analytic and policy paralysis left it open, even eager, for guidance; but its leaders had no notion whatsoever of other nations' experiences with the international financial community. Their ignorance proved to be decisive.

When Linh and Kiet took over the national economy's direction in 1985, they had already been well primed by Nguyen Xuan Oanh, and their definition of the role and potential of the market was by then so close to the IMF's that there was a certain inevitability about what followed. Throughout this entire period Linh, Kiet, and others accepted Oanh's advice, which was identical to the IMF's and World Bank's formula for all nations. His influence on them was indisputable: he was made director of Ho Chi Minh City's Economic Research Office, appointed to the National Assembly in early 1987, and later also became involved in investment and banking. He was unquestionably Vietnam's most prominent and important economist during these crucial years. While the IMF about this time was certainly more persuasive, if only because it promised loans and World Bank aid if its counsel were accepted, its views also coincided with Oanh's. What was most remarkable about him was not that he was a consummate opportunist – they exist everywhere, at all times – but that Communist leaders listened to him carefully and acknowledged the fact publicly. He was also a key link with the IMF.

The IMF blocked credits to Vietnam in 1985 because it failed to pay its arrears or adopt "a reasonable set of policies."[5] In August 1987, with its reform program capsizing and no alternatives, the Politburo accepted the IMF's advice to eliminate subsidies, impose budget controls, adjust the exchange rate and pricing system, and decentralize decision making. It also began to impose hospital and school fees and alter the state investment policy – in effect, it endorsed the entire IMF package, one that many countries are reluctant to accept, much less implement. It introduced a "contract responsibility system" for state-owned industry similar to the one China and the Soviet Union were then beginning to implement; I shall return to this crucial decision later in this chapter. At the end of 1987, Vietnam was again made eligible for loans, but before it could implement its pledges the Politburo's disastrous March 1988 currency reform triggered a fresh surge of inflation. The IMF then suspended loans and sent a delegation to Hanoi to tighten its conditions. Together they produced a plan. From this time onward, both the IMF and World Bank, as the Bank later phrased it, became continuously "active in a policy dialogue with the Government."[6]

Whatever the Communist party's rhetoric or its pretensions, Vietnam's economic and social direction since 1986 is comprehensible only in the context of the IMF's central influence. The party's ideologues still evoke Marx, Lenin, and Ho Chi Minh devoutly, but the IMF's inspiration has been far more decisive, and it has determined the nation's crucial priorities. When it came to interpreting the alleged "laws" the Politburo asserted existed in all economics, it asked the IMF to do so for the Communist party! In politics, no matter what ideology is proclaimed, what people do is infinitely more significant than what they say. Vietnam's economy halted its steep decline in 1989, but not because it acted as the IMF insisted. There were far more crucial factors at play, above all the end of the war in Cambodia, and had they not existed the depression would certainly have continued. I discuss them later in this chapter (pp. 43–9).

Most nations that agree to IMF conditions ignore them in part or whole once they receive their money. Had Vietnam done the same then it would have been normal behavior, save that the IMF makes loans conditional on the strict implementation of its program – which it waives only if there are political reasons to do so. Were Vietnam to falter, its access to funds would be suspended, and so it followed IMF directives loyally. The IMF is not trifled with lightly, and it has no reason publicly to defend a wayward socialist nation; its evaluation of Vietnam's record since 1987 is the most authoritative criterion for judging the Communist party's present economic and social policies. It also informs us about the extent to which the party has kept its compact with the people, one paid for with their suffering and blood beyond anyone's comprehension, and the intensity of its socialist commitments. The IMF's judgment also tells us where Vietnam is heading and the type of society that is emerging. Everything that follows in this book should be read with this pervasive reality in mind.

In late 1994 the IMF concluded that Vietnam had "made remarkable progress in the transition to a market-based economy" as it defined it.[7] At the end of 1995, its sister institution, the World Bank, surveyed the extent to which twenty-eight former (or, in two cases, present) "Communist" nations had conformed to its "cumulative liberalization index," which measures their total reforms. Vietnam was the sixth highest, far more "liberal" than now-capitalist Russia.[8] "Few economies in transition to market-oriented systems," the IMF wrote in July 1996 just as the party was renewing its devotion to Marxist-Leninist-Ho Chi Minh thought, "have achieved relative macroeconomic stability more quickly."[9] This entailed "lowering real labor costs, cutting back or eliminating subsidies to consumers and state enterprises, and reducing capital outlays." I will detail the specific effects of these far-reaching measures on the people later, but by 1996 even the IMF was concerned that, as in all the nations which destroy the social benefits that had accumulated under socialism, the program was "eroding popular support for the reform process" and "the will of the authorities to 'stay the course'."[10] Would *doi moi*'s political costs prove too high?

DEFINING MARKET SOCIALISM

Doi moi's intellectual synthesis produced uncomfortable dilemmas almost as soon as it was introduced. Attempting to reconcile its own disagreements rather than make its guidelines more precise, the Politburo since then has applied contradictory, ad hoc pot-pourri policies which confirm that it is comprised of men wholly unqualified for the vast authority they claim as their own in the name of the "proletariat." As the last Vietnamese troops withdrew from Cambodia and the USSR and the East bloc began to disintegrate, the central committee's crucial sixth plenum in March 1989 attempted to articulate a much more comprehensive basis for the economic hybrid which some dignified by calling it "state-initiated capitalism."[11] It issued a blanket account of past failures without seriously explaining their causes, or what had succeeded fairly well as opposed to not at all, and concluded that "the private, individual, small owner, and private capitalist economic forms are still necessary in the long run for the economy . . . in the structure of the commodity-based economy for the advance toward socialism."[12] A "planned commodity economy" would operate on market principles: ending subsidies, reforming the tax system, introducing tuition fees in schools, charging for hospitals and medical care, and the like.[13]

This definition, with modifications in detail but not in substance, has served since 1989 as the economy's theoretical goal and basic policy. But because it is so obviously vague and contradictory, even incomprehensible, the party's economic program remains far less important than the manner in which it is being implemented. I cannot stress sufficiently that it is only by looking at economic realities, and not its theory, that we can understand how Vietnam has developed since 1986. The Politburo's resolutions reflect the intense power struggles and compromises within its own ranks, and they are scarcely unavoidable deductions from abstract "laws," which cannot in any case be translated into specific strategies involving difficult choices. Even more important, those who greatly influence its declarations have remarkably little control over how they are implemented, and the differences are often decisive. The Politburo responds to political necessities, not economic problems. And it is precisely for this reason that it is increasingly ignored in daily life, which is irresistibly escaping the Politburo's control.

As I show in detail in the following chapters, in a domain where actions are infinitely more consequential than rhetoric, the International Monetary Fund has been the principal influence on Vietnam's policies since the late 1980s. Vietnam, even much more emphatically than most nations that have formally abandoned communism, has rigorously applied IMF-recommended macroeconomic policies, with profound consequences for the entire society and socialism. The result has been a quiet but profound revolution within the Communist nation, with the theorists on the Politburo – generally those with a strong socialist orientation – increasingly resembling Delphic oracles while those pro-"market" members in charge of the administrative decision-making bodies exercise real power. By 1995 this ever-widening gap between theory and power, between the men of ideas and those of action, had become too huge to ignore, producing the first real political crisis within the innermost ranks of the party's leadership. I discuss this crucial impasse in Chapter 6.

However sincerely the Vietnamese party believes that its very existence guarantees a market economy will culminate in a socialist society, there can be no doubt whatsoever that since at least 1989 its leaders have encouraged or tolerated the creation of an economic structure that by an objective definition will be capitalist insofar as large-scale private property is legitimized, wealth redistributed, and an exploited proletariat created. Their assumption, like those of China's leaders, is that this unprecedented hybrid social system can cope with growing economic power in the hands of new elites and avoid the conflicts inherent in any class society. That the party's hegemony by itself assures the continuation of socialism ignores both the question of social equity and the growing autonomy of the provincial party bureaucracies – which for practical purposes creates a functional split in the organization. The Politburo is thereby risking both socialist objectives and the very future of its Leninist organization at one and the same time. Its great gamble is increasingly likely to fail.

While significant elements within its leadership have increasingly opposed these changes, and verbal concessions have been made to the critics, the combined direction of the party's actions and statements is unmistakable. By the mid-1980s it was clear that major innovations in the economy were imperative. The real issue, ideally, should have been the social organization that future development takes, for existing state firms could have been reformed within a socialist framework which accepted certain preconditions for productivity, and according to guidelines that do not incorporate the IMF's "market" premises. But in practice, as I detail later in this chapter, a basic struggle emerged between two options, either of which can only result in one or another form of private control over industry – and socialism in its original definition as public ownership for social ends is relentlessly being abolished. As in China, only the rhetoric will remain unchallenged.

The Politburo's dismantling of a socialist economy that began in the late 1980s, ostensibly in the name of efficiency, ignored the state's much larger role elsewhere in Asia. Vietnam public enterprises' share of the gross domestic product (GDP) – about one-quarter – in 1989 was only equal to its role in capitalist Malaysia. Its policy was in reality a result of pressure from the IMF, which promised loans in return for concessions that outside bankers considered "amazing."[14] It took four more years for the World Bank actually to grant them, but meanwhile the IMF and the Bank influenced the Politburo profoundly. Even planning for a stock exchange began. In March 1989 the party endorsed the principle of transforming loss-making state establishments into "state capitalist enterprises" that might be loaned or sold to what were ambiguously referred to as "private collectives."[15] Because the term "capitalist" shocked some traditionalists, it was used sparingly until 1996, when the crucial June party congress resolved that the "state capitalist economy . . . plays an important role in . . . the socialist construction undertaking."[16] Descriptions such as these are not meant to clarify complex and important issues but only to reconcile differences among the leaders. On its face value they can mean almost anything.

The party resolved that Vietnam will develop a "multisectoral economy and give various economic components and business establishments more headway to develop quickly ... the state [will] regulate and lead the market economy to develop further in accordance with ... socialist orientations."[17] Implicitly, in accordance with World Bank advice, state economic activities were to concentrate on loss-making infrastructure projects. The "equitization" of state firms was substituted for the term "privatization," which openly concedes that socialism is being abolished, but the party tamely endorsed the essential principle. A party that dialectically mobilizes the ostensible laws of Marxism-Leninism to justify capitalism will not be hindered by mere words; it has played fast and loose with all of them, and only its actions now matter. What is essential, a party spokesman wrote in March 1994, is that "we have completely eliminated the antipathy, prejudice, and prohibition against private capitalist and individual sectors, thus creating the conditions for all production forces to develop for the sake of the country and people."[18]

On the whole, however, the Politburo after 1988 consistently disparaged the existing state sectors and strongly encouraged the private economy, which it expected to become the principal impetus to economic growth. But the results (which I detail later, pp. 52–7) proved very different, and it took at least five years for it to even acknowledge – and only very partially at that – that its initial expectations were grossly flawed and that it had seriously underestimated the state sector's potential. In essence, the Politburo's predilection for the "market" has increasingly borne little relationship to economic experience. Just as the Leninist dogmas borrowed from the Soviet Union and China prevented it from comprehending the world realistically before 1986, its market illusions have obscured its perceptions since then. There has consistently been an enormous disparity between existing economic or social realities and their ideologically deduced definitions. In large part this is due to the fact that Vietnamese communism, which since its origins has always been intent on showing it was truly internationalist, never achieved a successful synthesis between foreign ideas and Vietnamese conditions.

The Communist party by the late 1980s had defined an ideological and institutional basis for abandoning almost entirely the legacies of its history and values before 1975.

Straddling two systems

Without any historical justification, the manner in which the party has redefined the concept of human economic behavior and motivation is based on a crude historical fiction, which conservative Chicago-school theorists and Reagan-Republicans also share, that also exculpates the corruption and social disorientation and disillusion it nominally deplores. Far more significant is the fact that the greatest problems confronted by most societies in this century were far less the result of modest growth rates than of social disorganization and the collapse of social values, including morale. An accounting fixation that measures the efficacy of an economy in short-term numbers fails utterly to understand those many nations that achieved quick economic successes but eventually were wracked by crises. Economic strategies are functional ultimately only in terms of social goals and priorities, and a society that is unstable internally will be crisis-prone. So-called market efficiencies are transient, and the fact that growth within a highly skewed income distribution carries intangible but eventually crucial liabilities, both in terms of class conflicts and underconsumption, eventually determines an economy's total performance. The very notion that there is something like an objective, inevitable economic law that transcends political values and class ends, and has a higher rationality, is an ideological myth that classical economics has preached with very uneven success – even among those who favor capitalism – for nearly 200 years. The Vietnamese party accepted this dangerously fatalist conception, which has sanctioned a determinism that absolves it from the need for sustained critical analyses and judgments.

Without exception, every economic program involves significant and unavoidable inefficiencies, but of radically varying sorts and consequences, and a crucial distinction between those on the Left and those on the Right is which social class they believe should suffer most from the problems that all economic strategies entail. Socialists, whether Leninists or Social Democrats, who ignore this reality cannot be trusted, and they can only betray their ostensible ideals.

The Politburo's new line, rather than coming to grips with Vietnam's complexities as specific, historically caused events – some of which were avoidable and others not – justified its essentially capitalist program in terms of ostensible Marxist global "laws." In fact, the Saigon regime could just as easily have implemented it, and it owed infinitely more to continuous IMF advice and pressure than to a sudden revelation from Leninist scriptures. These putative laws are intellectually disgraceful, simplify the world as badly as its mechanistic Marxist-Leninist strictures of the past, and only obfuscate issues and make positions dogmatic. This growing reference to "laws" began in the early 1980s, when so-called reformers favoring "market" and capitalist methods argued for their existence against the more traditional socialist assumptions and programs, which had scarcely evolved since the 1950s and were highly vulnerable. The fact that these sclerotic ideas required fundamental revisions made it easy for another erroneous strategy to replace them.

By 1989 it was common for party leaders to justify specific policies by asserting that they conformed, in Nguyen Co Thach's words, to "the objective law governing the economy," "general development laws of the world economy," and "universal laws of the commodity production."[19] The June 1991 congress criticized the party's earlier position as having "violated the law of objectivity" without explaining how a ruling party could take fifty years to discover such inviolable rules in Marx's writings.[20] What reliance on "the law of evolution" means, as an advocate of "low wages, good workers, and concessional taxes" stated it, is that "only the strong development of the production force can create the absolutely necessary conditions for socialism."[21] "It is an illusion to wish to advance directly to socialism without going through the stage of capitalist development. . . . Realities do not allow us to advance directly to socialism. . . . Allowing the capitalist factor to reach a certain level of development during the transition period is an objective issue," in the words of one writer, and one presumably can no more argue with what is "objective" than to alter nature.[22] This mechanistic, necessitarian vision of economics evokes the virtues of "competition" and is grounded far more on Ricardo than on Marx or Lenin.[23] It has also led the party into a bottomless analytic trap, producing more dogmatism instead of wisdom.

In January 1994, after the party had been in power for a half-century and had consistently claimed infallibility throughout that time, Do Muoi confessed that "the building of socialism, however, is still new to us," and that by reading Marxist and "especially Leninist thoughts on a new economic policy and the state-managed capitalism . . ., this will help invent new forms of transition."[24] This vision of history as being governed by laws preordained to attain socialism regardless of expedient tactical deviations along the way, as if there were no relationship between means and ends, is being utilized to condone ethically and politically irresponsible policies that are morally and intellectually delegitimizing the party both in the eyes of the people and of many of its oldest members.

In pre-1985 Marxist reasoning, based on historical experiences that have caused innumerable non-Marxists to come to the same conclusion, an ascendant class that dominates the economy will eventually control the state as well. Such a rising class has no vested interest in nominal Communist control, since the party is the only force that can challenge it, and when the opportune time comes, it will – as occurred in the USSR – seek to translate its economic interests into political power. The Vietnamese party has, in effect, renounced the truism that social and economic relations define politics by arguing that "the leadership of the party is the decisive factor in maintaining a socialist orientation for our market economy and the entire development of our country."[25] In a word, the party plus capitalism equals socialism. But such a hybrid – "market-oriented socialism," or "market mechanism with state management" – has never existed anywhere, if only because the very notion of capitalism based on free markets is a historical fiction concocted by nineteenth-century ideologists; yet if this synthesis fails to succeed, then it is far more likely that the party will be destroyed and Vietnam will also go the way of the East bloc nations.[26] In any case, a party that confesses it erred seriously during most of its history will scarcely convince anyone that it has either the legitimacy or aptitude to rule any longer. To retain power under such circumstances, it can only employ repression, and at best it could succeed for only a limited time.

This policy of a state-managed capitalism, eventually to include a stock market and laws appropriate for a capitalist economy, has been increasingly institutionalized since 1986. By the end of 1990, the party was committed formally to three types of ownership: that by the peasants, essentially involving private land holdings; private property, which it predicted would expand greatly and create the most growth; and collective or state ownership, which surprisingly proved to be the most dynamic sector despite the Politburo's reluctance until 1995 to acknowledge it. From its inception, it seriously failed to identify the potentially most important sources of strength within the economy. As has been so often the case in history, leaders followed rather than led events. Vietnam's economic achievements since 1989 have not been the result of planning but of largely unanticipated developments and a fortunate conjunction of circumstances, by far the most important of which was the end of the Cambodian war. Instead, the Communists erroneously attribute their success to the market.

The 1992 constitution, which is a collection of specific legislation rather than a permanent state charter, failed to codify this potpourri into a coherent, consistent form; resistance from more traditional socialists required sufficient loopholes for it to remain ambiguous on many crucial matters. Since the liabilities of such vague regulations are all too obvious, and the state has so far been unable to reconcile them, it is the actual implementation of the new economic program – above all its corruption, fraud, and smuggling – that has defined largely what the constitution functionally means.

Merging the myth of the "market" and all the shibboleths of nineteenth-century laissez-faire capitalism with the panoply of inherited Marxist-Leninist rhetoric has produced an analytic and intellectual muddle, making the party's original socialist views largely irrelevant since *doi moi* was initiated. This promiscuous eclecticism makes it possible for astonishingly contradictory statements to come simultaneously from a group of men of approximately equal political power, and some leaders' ideas are merely crude attempts to reconcile both socialist and capitalist ideas – if only to compromise their differences – in the quixotic hope of attaining the alleged assets of both with none of their liabilities. Indeed, party leaders and writers have increasingly publicly acknowledged this obvious, pervasive confusion and "that it is not easy to set a clear cut boundary between socialist disorientation and a firm grasp of socialist orientations at the initial stage."[27] This disorientation has led to a breakdown in the way Vietnam now functions. In fact, the titular rulers are becoming increasingly irrelevant to the way people in and out of government behave in practice, with grave implications for the party's future.

Meanwhile, the party after 1992 restated and somewhat refined its earlier decrees, but its vague policies' negative social consequences are mushrooming even as it preaches the utopian position that the new entrepreneurs should behave like selfless revolutionaries. The 1994 party conference, while reiterating its earlier nominal socialist position, also formally endorsed much of the IMF–World Bank's advice. These organizations advocate a much smaller state sector that concentrates on those largely unprofitable transport, human, and energy infrastructure developments which are essential for private economic growth, and the party implicitly accepted this restricted role and the eventual privatization of profitable state industries. On the whole, its positions have been mutually at odds, and since 1993 they have reflected an increasingly basic, irreconcilable conflict within the party's leadership on fundamental economic goals. More important, as I detail later in this chapter, it is precisely the state sector that the IMF has proposed to dissolve which has enabled the economy to develop since 1989.

Given the deepening impasse among the leaders, who are unanimous only on the need to maintain their own political hegemony rather than how to resolve crucial and difficult policy challenges, Vietnam is drifting aimlessly in many crucial social and institutional areas. The Politburo is guiding the nation less and less, but no other body is able to do so. Notwithstanding impressive economic growth statistics, there is a profound crisis in motivation and morale within the party and among the population. Along with unresolved economic problems, it is eroding the nation's social fabric. After 1994, the possibility of this impasse leading to an institutional crisis within the Politburo and party began to increase dramatically, and the June 1996 congress was the first public expression of a conflict comparable in many ways to that of the Soviet Union during its final years.

THE RESULTS: PARADOXES OF SUCCESS

The Politburo embarked on its *doi moi* strategy in 1986 with the same uncritical faith in the IMF and World Bank market ideology as it had earlier placed in Soviet and Chinese advice, and it expected the private sector to become the principal motor of expansion. It was, for practical purposes, oblivious to the intimate relationship between long-term economic development and the investment in human capital. But after 1989, economic events failed largely to conform to the scenarios it had anticipated or the World Bank and IMF had promised, but still there was rapid growth as measured by strict accounting criteria. Indeed, by 1991 the increasing disparity between facts and its preconceptions had become immense, but rather than leading to an economic break-down, which is usually the case when plans prove irrelevant, the party kept incrementally adapting to each challenge, depriving it of any coherent plan or vision – including a false one – on which to base its planning. It had abandoned socialism as the basis for its economic program but yet it gradually realized that the so-called market solution was not working either. Nonetheless, the economy in its own fashion kept growing, inhibiting any impulse to make major changes.

Despite its pervasive confusion, the party has succeeded temp-orarily, to an unprecedented extent, by eclecticism and because of factors largely beyond its control: luck it wishfully believes will continue in the future. Its ultimate problem is that high growth's profoundly corrosive effects on the party and society in general were also unanticipated, and when its good fortune runs out – as inevitably it must – it will be left with many of the worst aspects of both socialism and capitalism as well as the negative residues of ten years of uncontrolled development.

Although Vietnam's economy has grown rapidly since 1988 if considered in the aggregate, the major problems with the available data and complexity of the causes make its success much less impressive than the party declares it to be. For the party's new economic policy was not the principal cause of growth: the lifting of the international blockade imposed after the invasion of Cambodia and the remarkable success of its oil industry explain most of it. Without these two crucial factors interacting the economy would have continued to decline, and it would have improved even if a "market" strategy had not been adopted. In fact, 1985 (before the new line was enacted) was the second-highest gain of any year between 1984 and 1991. Industrial output after 1988 was about twice as rapid as in the far larger agricultural sector, and the total gross domestic product (GDP) growth rate increased from 5.1 percent in 1990 to 8.8 percent in 1994 and 9.5 percent in 1995. When the party endorsed the market line it did so after mercilessly denigrating the state-owned economy, and it predicted that the private sector would be the principal source of growth. On the basis of reported data, however, state industry's expansion since 1990 has been about twice as fast as that of the nonstate sector, although without oil it would have declined sharply in 1990 and oil has grown much more slowly since 1991–2. But the net result has been that the state's share of both industries and services (and therefore the entire GDP) has increased appreciably – from 32.5 percent in 1990 to 40.2 percent in 1994.[28]

The party also failed to anticipate that the "private" sector in Vietnam would, as in the rest of Southeast Asia, be overwhelmingly Chinese-dominated and therefore emphasize marginal, less-productive, and mobile activities that produce quick returns and remain highly liquid. About 60 percent of the private sector is now Chinese-controlled, equivalent to roughly their share throughout Southeast Asia, and whatever private development occurs will entail this constraint.[29] But the Chinese way of doing business is often invisible and impossible to document. As I show later (pp. 49–52), the result is that a great deal of foreign investment and trade does not move through channels the state can control – and tax. The seemingly superior growth of the state over private industry reflects this reality, because in fact both the private sector and foreign-owned companies underreport their performance – again to avoid taxes. They have done better, perhaps much better, than official data indicate.[30] There was simply no way that a "market" strategy could transcend the dominant Chinese role and create a durable, balanced foundation for economic development. That the majority of the Politburo ignored this self-evident, pervasive fact merely reveals how deductive and ideological its assumptions were from the inception.

While the data on inflation are not entirely consistent, there can be no question that the intolerable annual rate of about 700 percent in 1986 and 300 percent in 1988 fell to 36 percent in 1990, shot back up to 83 percent in 1991, and fell back to 14.5 percent in 1994 and 13.1 percent in 1995. Although the achievement is impressive whatever the cause, its success is mitigated by the fact that food is greatly underweighted in the official price index, which makes the data appear considerably better than the reality. For example, food prices in 1994 increased over three times more than all other goods; food comprises the larger part of consumer expenses, especially for the poor. Because of this continuing pressure, the population remains very wary, and hoarding remains a problem.[31]

Given the collapse of Soviet and East bloc aid and trade after 1990, the Vietnamese improvised successfully until about 1995 by relying largely on exports to convertible currency areas to pay for imports, but there were serious problems in the way they did so. Exports grew moderately from 1979 to 1987, but given the world trade boycott even this was an accomplishment. Vietnam was extremely fortunate that the boycott ended just as Russian aid was slashed; had it not, their exports certainly would not have tripled between 1988 and 1993, thereby more than compensating for the aid cuts. This surge was the consequence of their new diplomatic policy, not some alleged "market" strategy. The Politburo has never acknowledged this primary fact, and it attributes growth erroneously to factors which it argues vindicate its wisdom. Events prove just the opposite.

By far the single most important reason for this export success was again also coincidental: oil (which was the result only of highly competent policies initiated over a decade before *doi moi*) increased in output ten times between 1988 and 1994 to become the single most important export after 1990.[32] With world prices rising in the wake of the Gulf crisis, oil's contribution to the state's revenue was crucial. Had the Cambodian war not ended, exports could not have grown so dramatically. Next came greatly increased rice exports, mainly to China, which rose fairly quickly but carry a very high domestic social price and are also burdensome to the balance of trade (all of which I detail in Chapter 4). Oil is about twice as important as rice. Since it is the only item capable of rapid increases, Vietnam has forced its rice exports to gain exchange for imports, but at the cost of reducing internal consumption – which is already far too low.

These improvisations worked fairly well for several years and certainly cushioned the potentially disastrous shock from the loss of East bloc aid, but the state began increasingly to lose control of trade, especially via smuggling; the 1993 official trade deficit of $655 million increased to $900 million the next year, by which time the nation's international payments balance was very serious. In 1995, the deficit leaped to $2.3 billion – the largest since the end of the war and for which no solution can or will be found. If smuggling is included, it was nearly twice as high. Its 1996 official deficit was projected to be two-thirds higher yet. As a percentage of the GDP, Vietnam's trade balance was favorable in 1990–2 but careened to –4.5 percent in 1993 and –17 percent in 1996. Its external debt as a percentage of its gross national product (GNP) in 1994 was already 161 percent.[33] *Doi moi* has placed Vietnam deeply in the debt trap, along with some of the world's most venal, poor nations, and it is therefore increasingly vulnerable to the dictates of the IMF and the world's bankers. While its traders have made fortunes, Vietnam is imposing ever-greater social costs on the people for the haphazard way in which the economy has evolved since 1989.

Vietnam's payments deficit is only one major problem in a series of growing interlocking fiscal difficulties that have accumulated, and a crisis in any one could easily trigger a chain reaction. One key link in this ominously fragile situation is its banking system, which after 1990 grew precipitously but with few controls over loan practices. By the summer of 1996 its mounting problems, especially among the private banks, had become too great to ignore: bad debts were rampant, accounting was lax, and rules routinely ignored. The state banks' health, while apparently not so precarious, was shrouded in mystery, but their unrecoverable loans, a confidential central bank report concluded in mid-1996, had reached "an alarming level."[34] Loose credit had encouraged rapid growth, but at a price that has yet to be calculated.

Whatever temporary good fortune Vietnam had, it was not matched by its internal fiscal position, although the state sector's growing share of the economy provided it with an important respite. When the Politburo after 1986 expected the private sector's proportion of the GDP to grow, it ignored the fact that it would be far more difficult to tax than state enterprises; had state industry not done so well there would have been a budgetary crisis much sooner and it would have been far worse than the present serious problem. The state sector accounted for two-fifths of the GDP in 1994 but contributed two-thirds of the government revenue.[35] Since the private sector has always been grossly under-taxed, a fact very difficult to reverse, Hanoi's new and growing fiscal difficulty since 1993 has been principally with the provincial parties. Indeed, it is their very large measure of administrative autonomy that poses the most immediate and serious challenge to the Politburo on every level of the economy, for many of the local bureaucracies have – as in China – increasingly become massively corrupt fiefdoms.

Hanoi's relations with the provincial parties is complicated because the war effort, with its emphasis on decentralized self-sufficiency, after 1959 obligated it to assign to them a great deal of functional authority. Local and provincial units created most of the state enterprises, and over time local party officials developed power bases independent of the central government – and increasingly in competition with it. Vietnam never attempted to impose mandatory controls on the Soviet or Chinese scale. Hanoi's plans were often treated quite casually, and during the war it neither could nor wished to do anything about it; and later it was unable to do so. After 1979, the provinces created their own trading operations and assumed considerable influence over foreign exchange earnings. When the Politburo embarked on *doi moi* in 1986, it had already lost a significant measure of authority over the economy it set out to reform – and many of the developments that have mocked it since then reflect this reality. While the economy and state sector appear to have grown statistically, numbers fail to reveal the extent to which the Politburo is increasingly losing power to autonomous regional party leaders.

The state's revenue as a share of the GDP has grown dramatically since 1990, and its budget deficits, while they sometimes fluctuate to high levels, at first sight do not look insurmountable. The core problem for Hanoi is to collect the taxes gathered in the provinces, and most data do not clarify an absolutely fundamental problem: which Communists control the budget. This decentralization of power also explains why its moralistic exhortations on every conceivable social, ideological, and economic topic fail to alter the reality. Ironically, the uncontrollable bureaucratic frankenstein that the party itself created is now a crucial source of its own paralysis. For this reason the Politburo quixotically hopes to use the "mass line" (which I discuss in the next chapter) to impose discipline over a party structure that is increasingly out of control.

As in China a decade earlier, since 1990 the Politburo has attempted to win the cooperation of the provincial parties on revenue sharing, offering an incentive system which legalizes hitherto unauthorized withholdings. If they send specified sums or shares to Hanoi, they may keep whatever they collect in excess of them. These efforts to control taxes have largely failed, and the Politburo has increasingly attacked the fact that "within some departments and provinces, sectionalism still prevails."[36] In the spring of 1996, by which time the budget deficit had become "a burning problem" and risen to the highest percentage of the GDP since 1992, Hanoi literally pleaded with the provinces to consent to an incentive-based revenue-sharing scheme.[37] The likelihood of their implementing an agreement is slight: the highly centralized party increasingly exists as an abstraction, the residue of a protracted, heroic conflict that evoked its members' and the people's maximum efforts. It is dissolving amidst the entrepreneurial ethos it has encouraged, war fatigue, and the contradictions inherent in its own organizational structure. The masses were never permitted to control the functional organization of the "party of the proletariat," with its Leninist centralizing pretensions, and increasingly the Politburo cannot do so either.

Given its swollen budget deficit and rising balance-of-trade deficit, there are many ways Vietnam could lose control of the economy: it may have to borrow much more abroad, which would be onerous even if it finds lenders; or it may have to risk renewed inflation. Any combination of fiscal problems could intersect to initiate a crisis and endanger its progress until now. Financially, it is in a trap – one of many confronting it. There has been economic success, but it has not come easily and Vietnam's eventual losses, which it must confront very soon, could be very high.

Foreign investment: the elusive dream

When Vietnam embarked on its market strategy, a crucial premise of the IMF–World Bank ideological litany which it uncritically accepted was that its "comparative advantage" of extremely low wages would quickly integrate it into the "international division of labor." Large foreign investments would be attracted to it, and much of the capital it required for long-term development would soon come from abroad. This assumption, which still is a powerful influence among the so-called reformers who would eliminate the economic residues of socialism entirely so long as the party remains in power, proved both extraordinarily naive and dangerous from its inception. In reality, Vietnam has obtained only a few of the positive but many of the negative results of foreign investment, gaining the worst of both worlds.

The party's readiness to implement the IMF's advice on lowering labor and social costs shaped profoundly the economy's trajectory and its consequences for the people, and the meaning of socialism to their daily existence. Low real labor costs, as I shall detail later, were far less successful in attracting foreign investment than in making the domestic economy much more profitable. To the extent that this occurred because of the lowest wages in the region, the workers have ended up paying for much of Vietnam's economic progress. The question of equity, of course, is not whether a class is taxed but who gains the most from the economy's benefits. Workers are far easier to tax than peasants, or anyone else for that matter. Taxes can produce socially positive results – or gross exploitation. This vital decision on how to accumulate capital and manage the nation, the importance of which cannot be overemphasized, has suffused every aspect of Vietnam's economic and social life since 1986. Eventually, the very future of socialism is likely to reflect the basic choice as to who pays and, even more consequential, who receives. While it initially may appear like an economic decision, in the end such fundamental options inevitably are profoundly political if they hurt the people.

Corruption increasingly penetrates every dimension of the Vietnamese state, the vague and inconsistent legal and banking laws are a source of continuous frustration, local authorities routinely ignore Hanoi's guidelines and impose their own, housing and building prices are exorbitant, and executive living conditions difficult (notwithstanding a drove of golf courses charging astronomical fees). The transport and physical infrastructure is underdeveloped in most areas – liabilities that greatly offset among the lowest labor costs in all of Asia. The effects of all this have been reflected in actual foreign investment.

About $23 billion in foreign investment projects were approved through mid-1996, but only about one-fifth of this sum has been actually disbursed – and much less if the local partners' share in joint ventures is deducted. The difficulties confronting investors are legion, and major projects in regions that might indeed have helped economic development, such as refining, have been cancelled amidst much publicity. Attempts to sell bonds on the world market have also failed, and Vietnam has remained a marginal country for investors, especially European and Japanese. The promarket faction dominating the Politburo expects that foreign investors, creditors, and donors will provide $30 billion of the $50 billion investment capital Vietnam needs between 1995 and 2000 to achieve its growth target, but at the current rate it will be fortunate to obtain one-third of that amount.[38]

Vietnam embarked on its present economic strategy on the naive assumption that it would repeat the performances of the other Asian "tigers," as if they had developed in a vacuum. But as many have pointed out, Korea, Taiwan, and others were initially dependent on American economic aid and contracts for a sustained period, and the Cold War context that made such economic growth possible has largely disappeared in the midst of a debt crisis, excess global production capacity, and growing unemployment in the Third World. The Politburo has not been able to come to terms with the fact that Vietnam, proportionate to its population, has the lowest rate by far of foreign investment of any Asian nation – barely half of Sri Lanka's, the next lowest – and from this perspective its efforts have failed dismally until now. It is low even compared to the former Communist states that opened their doors at the same time. For it to rely on outsiders for development is a chimera. By 1996, many officials admitted publicly that attracting foreign capital was much more difficult than expected, and very well might not fulfill expectations. Meanwhile, it is optimizing the worst of both the capitalist and socialist alternatives while abandoning the assets of the latter, and the social costs of this approach are incalculable.

The Vietnamese quickly discovered that foreign businesses frequently utilize old technology, often capitalized at much greater than its real value, and many are ruthless exploiters of labor out to enrich themselves quickly. Six export processing zones were initiated with great fanfare, despite the fact that similar zones elsewhere in Asia have generally not been successful, and granted special tax and other concessions; they were immediate failures and several are on the verge of dissolution. By 1996, foreign investment had created employment for only 90,000 people, about 2 percent of the total working non-agricultural labor force.

Convinced by them that it could prosper if it did so, Vietnam accepted and assiduously implemented virtually all World Bank and IMF advice on crucial legal and institutional prerequisites for investors. It has, in their opinion, moved quickly, "liberalizing" much more than most nations that have explicitly abandoned socialism.[39] But Vietnam's so-called foreign investment is highly complex. For one thing, over two-thirds of it, especially in oil and industry, has gone into joint ventures with state firms despite a legal and administrative structure that is ostensibly oriented to those true entrepreneurs prepared to risk initiating new industries rather than work through those already established. Oil firms have largely implemented their projects, but the vast bulk of the remaining investors, principally in manufacturing, tourism, and hotels, scarcely conform to the ideal image of foreign investors. An overwhelming portion are Chinese commercial interests, some of which worked under the Saigon regime, left after 1975 and are now returning to Vietnam; they usually collaborate with local ethnic Chinese, including relatives and friends. Taiwan, Hong Kong, and Singapore, therefore, are by far the three largest investors, and about 60 percent of all authorized investments so far have come from Asian nations, Japan excluded. Their unregistered investments, however, may be just as large, and they enter and leave the country at will.[40]

In this sense, much of Vietnam's foreign investment has meant Chinese re-entry in one form or another, and reintegration of the nation into the overarching web of ethnic Chinese business enterprise that rules Southeast Asia's economy. Combined with local Chinese domination of the private sector, Vietnam is in reality accommodating to the pervasively Chinese reality of East Asia, surrendering far less to the IMF's mythical international division of labor or "market" than to the Chinese way of business, which is geared to premises radically different than those of western market theory. It is oriented far less to basic longer-term industrial development than ventures that produce high returns and hard currency quickly – property, hotels, services and the like – which will soon become a drain on the nation's exchange reserves.

Prime Minister Vo Van Kiet is fully aware of this relationship, and the Chinese – mainly centered in Ho Chi Minh City, where the majority of investments go – justifiably consider him as their close ally. The question of foreign investment and trade is therefore inextricably linked to the status of local capitalists, who were, are, and will remain overwhelmingly Chinese. Encouraging domestic capitalists means, above all, reassuring the local Chinese that they can unleash their hidden capital and talents, as they have hesitantly begun to do. The party has therefore gone to some pains to restore their confidence, even returning most of the Mekong rice mills nationalized after 1975 to their original owners or their families. The implications of such measures for the peasants are potentially very great.

THE MYTH OF SOCIALIST INDUSTRIALIZATION: PRIVATIZING INDUSTRY

The Communist party has always declared that Vietnam will remain a socialist economy in fact as well as inspiration, and were it to abandon the raison d'être of its very existence it also would lose its fundamental ideological legitimacy. Indeed, it might even face open dissent within its own ranks, for a very significant section of the party, including a minority of the Politburo, retains a profound belief in socialist goals defined more generally than simply the party's control of power. Since the early 1990s they have been increasingly uncomfortable publicly with the vast changes that have altered every aspect of the society.

This internal constraint has made it inconceivable for Vietnam, just as it was impossible for the Soviet Union during its final years or China at the present time, to acknowledge publicly the already well-advanced fundamental transformation of its state-owned industries. This complex process is occurring in various ways that operate in tandem – some informal, others nominally illegal, and others sanctioned. Despite this, the party has declared it is committed to state-led industrialization operating along market lines. Many of the idealistic party members still sincerely believe it, and find it painful to confront reality; they retain the hope that what is universally described as unrelenting, growing corruption is merely an aberration – an exception rather than the rule. Meanwhile, for nearly a decade Vietnam has been undergoing exactly the same changes as occurred throughout the East bloc before and after the collapse of communism, and in China as well: a very extensive portion of the legally state-owned industries is being systematically privatized.[41] Because the party refuses even to acknowledge the fact that a massive transfer of property is taking place, no precise estimate of its magnitude exists. But it is by now common and widespread. State industry is following the same route as every other aspect of the economy: no matter what it is called, social ownership is irresistibly being dismantled – as effectively, indeed, as if the party's leaders proclaimed what they dare not: the abolition of socialism.

Vietnam's present privatization of industry – and its grand economic strategy – is the inevitable logic of its sustained imitation of Soviet and Chinese models. This dependency also left it susceptible to IMF and World Bank advice. Because of this inherently inappropriate way of deciding on issues fundamental to its future, Vietnam has confronted many surprises – some agreeable, others not – which neither the IMF nor the Chinese prepared them for. The Politburo since the end of the war has attempted to command the economy but essentially it never really controlled it or, even worse yet, fully comprehended it. Its ignorance has led to decisive errors.

Adapting successfully to the long liberation war's impact compelled Vietnam's state industry, as even the World Bank admits, "to improve managerial performance."[42] It was much more decentralized, and it surprised its critics and the advocates of a "socialist market economy," who expected that merely allowing private industry to exist would cause the capitalist "market" sector to flourish and outperform the state-owned enterprises (SOEs). But results since 1988 have reflected unique Vietnamese conditions, which advocates of the market did not comprehend at all, that favored the SOEs' growth and profit. These conditions also encouraged serious corruption.

The large majority of the SOEs belong to the district and provincial governments, which gives them significant political protection from Hanoi's discipline, and the central government owns mainly the larger capital-intensive firms. It also makes them more susceptible to cronyism and corruption. But while the SOEs play a major role as a share of the GDP, in 1989 they employed only about 8 percent of the labor force. The SOEs' potential, such as it was, had yet to be realized. But a strong residue of hostility to relying on the state sector still persists among a considerable number of party leaders and technocrats, who continue sharply to criticize the SOE performance and prefer to rely much less on them. The private sector, which largely meant Chinese entrepreneurs, was given unprecedentedly large scope for its activity. But, as everywhere else in the region, the Chinese are unwilling to concentrate on long-term industrial development.

The state enterprise reform of November 1987 allowed the SOEs far greater autonomy over production and business operations, including investments and subcontracting. "Socialist business accounting" was introduced, but some subsidies continued.[43] Subsequent decrees in 1991 and early 1992 allowed the SOEs even greater control over their assets, more leeway to sell, transfer, or liquidate fixed assets, and much larger scope for creating holding companies and foreign-financed joint enterprises – steps that eased the way for inside managers to enrich themselves.

Of about 12,300 state firms, approximately 5,000 were liquidated or allowed to become private after 1987, but this number comprised only 4 percent of all SOE assets. Despite IMF and World Bank pressure and its own differences, the Politburo decided that the SOEs as a whole should be reformed and given time to succeed. About 800,000 workers were dismissed between 1989 and 1993, direct state subsidies were virtually eliminated after 1989, and cut entirely in all indirect forms – such as cheap resources and credits – by 1992. Imitating South Korean, Chinese, and Russian models, the state also created conglomerates intended to coordinate all enterprises in major sectors, such as coal, steel, and machinery, although their precise function remains unclear either to the Vietnamese or to others. By mid-1995, eleven existed.

On the basis of the official data, whose serious limits I noted earlier, the SOE growth rate in industry, including construction, quickly exceeded the performance of the nonstate sector, often very dramatically. The SOEs grew an average 12.7 percent annually from 1990 through 1994, and nonstate industry only 6.4 percent. But taking the annual growth rate for all sectors of the economy over this period, state expansion outdistanced private enterprise by half – 9.6 versus 6.2 percent. The SOE share of industrial production therefore rose from 66.4 percent in 1989 to 71.3 percent in 1993, and higher since. SOE industry's proportion of the GDP rose from 14.4 percent in 1990 to 19.4 percent in 1994. Only in services (basically trade) has the nonstate sector performed significantly better, so that the overall state share of the GDP since 1990 has sharply increased. Even taking into account the limits of the statistics, the market's promised miracles did not materialize.[44]

SOE transfers to the budget between 1990 and 1995 increased by over six times, and by 1993 the subsidies to the SOEs amounted to only 1.4 percent of their payments to the state budget. The state sector, as the World Bank admitted, performed not only far better than any of the other Communist states "but is also remarkably good in comparison ... to the high performing SE sectors in Korea and Thailand."[45] This impressive achievement, notwithstanding the potentially fatal corruption associated with it or deleterious causes, which I detail later, is in stark contrast to the Chinese experience, much less the Russian, where the SOEs' role has declined dramatically.

Principally because of the SOEs, the state sector's contribution to total government revenues increased from 13 percent in 1986 to

52 percent in 1992 and 67 percent in 1994 – equivalent to about 11 percent of the entire GDP. Because of the state firms' relative prosperity, Hanoi's role in the economy, both real and potential, appears to have increased dramatically if one ignores entirely the internal character of a significant proportion of them, which makes state ownership more nominal than real. Putting this aside for the time being, in addition to spurring much higher growth, the SOEs have sustained the state budget. Revenues as a share of GDP rose from 14.7 percent in 1990 to 24.9 percent in 1995 only because the public sector paid its taxes.

An inherent liability of large private ownership is in efficient tax collection, which is difficult enough even in highly developed nations but virtually impossible elsewhere. Vietnam's farmers pay very little and there is no relatively simple way, as before *doi moi*, to collect their tax – thereby excluding roughly a third of the GDP. But private business tax evasion is rampant and blatant, and corruption among tax collectors aggravates the problem. Tax audits reveal that about half of the family businesses do not pay taxes at all, and they account for over half the sums owed.[46]

The SOEs' success has made any major changes of the state's role of fundamental importance to the very future of the socialist system, and it has greatly complicated the nature of the debate over privatization. Although politics and the desire to give state property cheaply to cronies or allies is often the true motive for privatization in most nations, public justifications for it have always claimed that SOEs are inefficient both intrinsically and compared to private ownership.

But Vietnam has shown that SOEs are far more functional, if not efficient in an objective technical sense, than private business, for both those who manage them and the state, whose ability to play a crucial fiscal role is now dependent wholly on both SOE growth and the payment of taxes. The honesty and integrity of the SOE system itself, much less the way it especially exploits its workers, is far less of an immediate dilemma for the party. In its own way, corrupt though it may be, the system works, and its success even on these profoundly compromised terms poses a much smaller immediate challenge than abolishing socialism formally as well as in essence – which is really what is irresistibly occurring, beneath a huge façade. For Vietnam to rely further on the private sector would certainly risk whatever crucial growth and revenue assets the fragile, poor nation now has at its command. Unlike China and

Russia, therefore, the fate of the state-controlled industries is fraught both with great danger and great promise. If the system is dismantled, either formally or informally, then the Communist party will play a much smaller economic role and confront a crisis of legitimacy, both in its relation to the people and within its own ranks – and its very fate may hinge upon it. Given the widespread corrupt informal privatization that is now occurring, such a crisis is sooner or later inevitable.

In essence, the party's principal challenge today is not simply to preserve the state industries but, above all, to make them also perform both honestly and equitably in relation to its workers. So far it has failed dismally.

Corruption and state industry

Vietnam's state industries in the years before *doi moi* were already beset by substantial and increasing corruption, mainly because the pricing system, a great deal of autonomy, and subsidies provided ample scope for it. *Doi moi* was also justified as an antidote to the venality that was leading to what some leaders described as a new "ruling class."[47] But it was quixotic to imagine that industrial managers, many of whom were already dishonest or corruptible under the old system, would suddenly become more honest if they were given far greater freedom. But in firms producing half the SOE output, managers after 1987 were responsible entirely for growth and profits, with the state receiving only a fixed sum in the form of taxes and the like. "Socialist accounting" was supposed to lead to efficiency as measured in profit, and this could be achieved in various ways: the technology, marketing, and production processes could be modernized and improved, but this required both substantial capital investments and expertise, which the managers did not have; or costs could be slashed with little or no change in these areas, and the only practical way of doing so quickly was by lowering workers' real wages. The government accepted the IMF's advice that this policy be adopted, and when firms that had previously been bailed out with state funds suddenly became profitable it was precisely for this reason. The SOEs' success has depended largely on taxing the workers, who, in effect, now subsidize them.

Because this arrangement has produced revenue for the state, the managers have been left virtually uncontrolled. It is, however, an open invitation to corruption. As managerial autonomy to engage in joint ventures and other deals expanded along with profits, new opportunities for corruption increased also, but no change was made in the state's already very lax accountability and supervision system. In practice, "socialist accounting" meant no accounting at all. Auditing procedures were finally issued in early 1996, but they have yet to be implemented.[48] Intrinsic in the very structure of the SOE strategy was the great potential for what the World Bank euphemistically calls "spontaneous privatizations."[49] Essentially, the Politburo rented its SOEs to the managers with astonishingly few conditions, and they stood to become rich from them if they made profits without subsidies.

There is always a functional utility to any arrangement that produces short-term results, but the party's fundamental dilemma is that it is committed to creating an egalitarian society, which is its very raison d'être – and this is exactly what its uncontrolled SOE reorganization, among many things, has prevented it from doing. All Communist societies in the transition toward the "market" suffer from the inherent contradiction between their socialist ideology and the acquisitive, individualistic behavior they urge people to pursue. Vietnam, like China, is encouraging all the people to become rich but it is providing only a tiny minority with the opportunities to do so – thereby sanctioning most of their actions. This obvious tension has profoundly confused both the masses and the party, disillusioning both.

Since the managers have had virtually free rein over the disposal of their company assets, they, their families, and cronies have exploited their opportunities aggressively. De facto privatization, essentially similar to that in Russia and especially China, is already well advanced. As the World Bank described it in 1996, "assets or income flows have slipped out of state hands and into private control, if not outright ownership, through a variety of methods. These transfers are often illegal and widely resented."[50] More important in terms of its potential, the vast majority of the approximately 1,200 foreign investment projects signed by mid-1995 are joint ventures with state enterprises, and they have enabled far more corruption among SOE managers than would have been possible without access to hard currencies and foreign markets. "Tens of thousands of cadres and civil servants," the party admits publicly, work for them, and "Not a few party members have become degraded because of the lure of money."[51]

Because Vietnamese critics of SOE corruption can write remarkably freely in the press, we know a great deal about it even though a precise estimate of its magnitude does not exist. Land rights are a major source of corruption, often involving large sums. SOEs use land rights as their principal capital contribution when they create joint ventures with foreign investors, but they can also borrow on it, transforming land into capital. One large published sample, however, has outlined the scope of all forms of dishonesty. An audit of ninety-nine state-owned companies, including thirty-five businesses and forty banks, found that in 1993 "most" had violated state regulations, lax as they were, regarding budgeted capital, receipts, and expenditures.[52] Abuses of land rights are rife, loans are given to family members and associates, state factories and workers are used for private production, houses and cars are purchased for private use, receptions and overseas travel are common – Vietnam's managers routinely exploit all of the countless perquisites and devices that their Chinese and Russian peers enjoy. The largest known scandal, in a firm that the party itself owned, became public in April 1996 and involved fifteen managers who cost their company nearly $40 million. Its director pocketed $5.5 million, including $270,000 for his mistress and $130,000 gambling losses. And as in China and Russia, SOE managers often establish private firms into which they channel important amounts of their state companies' funds and assets – "pseudo-private activities under their umbrella" is the World Bank's description of them – and the so-called private sector is to a significant degree really an extension of SOE managerial entrepreneurship.[53] In fact, many of the 5,000 SOEs that were ostensibly abolished after 1991 became the private property of SOE directors.[54] Unlike in China, the SOEs have prospered, but the potential for corruption was inherent in them from the inception and far exceeds the fraud that reforms were supposed to abolish. The cost to morale, social equity, and socialism's very objectives has been incalculable.

Legal privatization: the Politburo confronts the managers

Vietnam is well along the path of privatizing its industrial assets in practice, and there is a huge disjunction between the way it has occurred and the Politburo's original plans. By late 1993, it believed, in Do Muoi's words, in "many circumstances, the state property belongs to no one," workers and officials had no "incentive" to see a firm develop, and what was required to end losses, corruption, and much else were reforms similar to those in agriculture.[55] Shares might be given to workers, but also sold to private interests to raise capital; the extent to which each might occur was left unspecified. By then the IMF and the World Bank, now permitted by the United States to expand loans to Vietnam, were aggressively advocating privatization and confidently expected that after a trial it would "be pursued more broadly" among profitable companies.[56] The January 1994 party conference endorsed a "shareholding enterprise system," and while workers and personnel were mentioned as the initial privileged owners, "private" and "other" shareholders were to be very much a part of the new formula.[57] Vietnam would develop a "multisectoral economy and give various economic components and business establishments more headway to develop quickly . . . the state [will] regulate and lead the market economy to develop further in accordance with . . . socialist orientations."[58] Implicitly, in accordance with World Bank advice, state economic activities will concentrate on loss-making infrastructure projects.

Since the party had already redefined Marxist-Leninist dialectics to assert that its laws objectively necessitated a capitalist stage, it decided to make privatization more palatable by describing it as "equitization." The Politburo's line, in this as in so many other areas, conflicts baldly with a reality that has largely escaped its control. In principle, the crucial June 1996 party congress reiterated its continuing support for the principle of privatization in various forms. It has done so less because it believes in it than because the international banks insist upon it, and its ideological rhetoric cannot conceal its astonishing opportunism.

But should Vietnam privatize industry in the legal manner the World Bank advocates, then those managers who already possess a large measure of control over it, along with their political allies, families, and the social and political networks of which they are often an integral part, will be threatened. They have therefore opposed privatization, as the World Bank explains it, "because continued state ownership preserves the ambiguous property rights that allow profit shifting, tax evasion, and asset looting, largely for the benefit for the incumbent managers."[59] It is a consummate irony that they are defending their gigantic thievery of socialist institutions in the name of socialism itself!

For the Bank and its Vietnamese allies, the question of privatization does not involve greater efficiency, since the existing arrangement is increasingly profitable (ignoring its high social costs), or even whether it should occur – for informal privatization is well along already. Basically, the issue is who will personally gain most from it and whether the managers of the SOEs, in the guise of public servants, will become, as in China, the leading economic plutocracy. Those who advocate privatization as the World Bank and IMF propose it have diverse motives, but virtually no one in the party has addressed the most immediate crucial problem, which is how to transform the SOEs into genuine socialist entities. The options, as presented so far, have been confined to two approaches to privatization, neither of which is compatible with equity and social justice. In both cases, socialism will certainly disappear.

The numerous official critics of the SOEs have advocated privatization because they allegedly are not profitable and, as on most topics, they produce false data to support their conclusions. In 1993, the IMF claims, 10 to 15 percent of the firms were losing money, but some party spokesmen assert that 20 to 25 percent, even 35 percent, is the valid figure. Both are wrong, for the loss-making firms' assets represented a tiny proportion of the total – as I note above, the SOE payments to the state in 1993 were about seventy-five times greater than their subsidies.[60] Essentially, they have argued on the grounds of efficiency taken from the irrelevant IMF–World Bank theoretical model. The debate has evolved within a very narrow and misleading framework in which each faction's conservative and avaricious ulterior motives are obvious.

But World Bank and IMF influence on some Politburo market advocates and many of Hanoi's technocrats has been profound and intellectually decisive, and Vietnam in 1992 and 1993 introduced its first privatization (always termed "equitization") measure just as the SOE managers were beginning to reap large rewards. The plan's structure was in essence similar to the Russian program and would have quickly resulted in managerial takeovers – loans for it were offered at little cost – but the managers had already extensively "spontaneously" privatized the SOEs and had little more to gain. They therefore successfully opposed privatization from the inception, and by mid-1995 only nineteen of over 6,000 SOEs had applied for it, and of these only three completed the process.[61]

"Legal" privatization has been stymied, regardless of the party's nominal commitment or the gestures it has made to implement it. The SOEs in most regions have strong links with the local political authorities, a goodly number of whom, as in China, have shared in the spoils and now pose a formidable obstacle to the Politburo's ambitions to regain full control over the industrial economy. Ironically, many of those who claim that they wish to save socialist industry have done the most to despoil it. The Politburo has therefore made a concerted – but so far vain – effort to reassert state control over the SOEs, which it is increasingly losing to its managers and the provinces. The Politburo's dilemma is identical to that of the party center in China. Having allowed so much functional power to escape from it, it aspires to put the genie back in the bottle. It now hopes halfheartedly that legal privatization and a stock market may enable it to do so. But its powerful opponents have stalemated its effort. The Politburo's proposals are even less likely to control state industry because its option to the present corrupt informal privatization is not socialism but an arrangement that will be – as in Russia and China – at least as corrupt as the status quo. This tawdry rivalry is only inexorably further delegitimizing the Communist party and abolishing what remains of socialist institutions in Vietnam. Only the rhetoric remains as strong as ever!

The government – again with IMF encouragement – has therefore consistently endorsed the idea of a stock market and shareholding system that presumably would make privatization more feasible and allow Hanoi to assert its control over the SOEs. Its effort has so far been a total failure because of the obvious impossibility of creating a genuine capital market in one of the world's poorest countries. At the same time, in January 1995 Hanoi established a new office to monitor the SOEs more closely, and it aspires to obtain the power to hire and fire managers. It has also floated proposals – which bear the unmistakable markings of the IMF – for a radically innovative form of privatization that would challenge the managers directly and whose consequences would be unique even by Chinese or Russian standards. As first presented, privatization would sell shares not only to managers and workers, as elsewhere, but also allow "other parties with a

strong interest in the companies, such as employees of the controlling ministries, [to buy] at sharply discounted prices and through
concessional loans of up to D5 million."[62] As this approach
evolved and became much more complex and ambitious, it also
added the idea of comprehensive management councils, perhaps
with the eleven or more existing enterprise groupings or conglomerates as their basis, which essentially would be run by state
ministries in Hanoi and guide integrated production and development strategies, the distribution of profits, and the like – "economic managers" as differentiated from the "commercial managers" who now actually run the SOEs. However tentative the
organization structure, the project is inspired by the astonishing
principle that "the state as owner is a very abstract idea."[63]

The ministry officials participating in this profoundly ambiguous scheme would not only be in a position to reassert control over
the present managers but "they will own some of the assets that
the state has entrusted to the state enterprise that they are
managing through the management council. In this sense, they are
actual owners just like other shareholders in the state enterprises."[64] While the extent of their possible ownership is left
vague, there is no question that the ministry officials would
become owners – ostensibly on behalf of the central government –
at little, if any, cost. They would wear two hats: one as state
officials, the other as shareholders. The very first privatization
implemented actually transferred the company to ministry officials in charge of the sale![65] Given this combination of state power
and personal incentives, the existing managers would immediately be challenged and the diversion of profits into the hands of
government bureaucrats–capitalists would alter profoundly their
control over the SOEs. They naturally oppose privatization, with
the protection of socialism as their ostensible reason!

Vietnam is not preserving the state industrial sector at the present
time, and for it to tolerate the status quo is to sustain the de facto
privatization that is already well advanced. But regardless of
whether the World Bank plan is implemented *or* the status quo is
retained, the state sector will be eliminated. Both alternatives
amount to abandoning the essence and purpose of the state's
ownership of industry.

Given the tremendous difficulties that any sort of change

entails, the party's temptation has been to tolerate a basically corrupt system that has been very successful in the short run in raising production and state revenues. Such a solution maintains an increasingly uneasy compromise within the leadership and permits its pretensions to be the ruling body to be maintained. Its grave danger is that the managers of "state industry" will continue to exploit and control its resources and sooner or later inevitably become an autonomous group with both privilege and great influence – and therefore power. Given their economic leverage and political linkages, these managers can develop into a decisive force in national political and economic affairs – as important as the big industrial managers in the Soviet Union were in deciding the fate of Gorbachev after 1987 (and of Yeltsin in 1992), when they demanded and obtained a fundamental change in his economic strategy. When the Politburo in June 1996 chose to allow the managers to pursue their present role just to sustain the fragile consensus within its own ranks, it also elected a high-risk strategy – the end results of which it can neither predict nor control. It would have been far more prudent, not to mention principled, for it to confront this potential challenge sooner rather than later; the longer it postpones doing so the more formidable the problem will become. Indeed, it will only become increasingly impotent over time to reverse events.

Vietnam, like China, may possibly sustain a corrupt and inequitable economy for some years yet, although this is far from certain. What it cannot do is to preserve the Communist party morally in the eyes of the people, or those of many of its own members, who are becoming utterly cynical about its pretensions in the face of the malaise now penetrating the entire political and economic structure. The total political implications of this profound transformation cannot be predicted exactly, but the eventual result is likely to be the disappearance of the party, for unlike the Russian party – which lost power before the worst economic disasters occurred and was thereby able to escape blame and revive itself – it intends to preside over a nation that is losing its identity and morale but is also beset by overwhelming, unresolved economic and social problems. To allow state industry to continue to be robbed will undermine the very principles of equity inherent in socialism, causing the society to polarize further along class lines and alienate the people. Inevitably, it will challenge the authority of the party itself.

Chapter 3

The Communist party's political crisis

Vietnam's political and economic problems since 1975 have inter-acted in myriad ways, compounding each other to produce a grave crisis within the Communist party – perhaps its last. Since all ruling Communist parties after 1988 were removed from power not by rebellions but principally because of their own intellectual and organizational transformation and the contradictions within the societies they produced, the development of comparable tensions in Vietnam makes the party's internal condition poten-tially decisive. Basic political changes in states usually evolve from major modifications in the underlying social forms and ideas, and they impinge on the fundamental issue of the control of power. Economies everywhere always reflect this pervasive reality. The party, at every level, is ceasing to conform to its original centralist ideals, and its profound demoralization has created a grave political crisis which impinges on the ultimate question of who rules, how, and – above all – why.

THE PARTY'S ORGANIZATIONAL AND MORAL IMPASSE

The liabilities inherent in being an authoritarian party in power have increased greatly since 1975. For decades, the Vietnamese party, unlike other Communist parties, consistently attempted to reconcile the profound tension between being a mass party in reality and Leninist in theory, but in practice being ruled by a small self-perpetuating Politburo whose preeminent half-dozen members refused to entrust party members with formal decision-making authority. But Vietnam's Politburo structure was a supremely successful adaption to a complex, protracted war against two mighty enemies, and so long as the war's exigencies justified its role, it could effectively and legitimately fend off demands for democratization. From its inception, it defended its position not on pragmatic grounds, which were credible, but as the personification of the proletariat's rule over the party, even though openly admitting it was itself comprised of intellectuals who became "leaders of the working class . . . with a working class consciousness and position" for reasons scarcely more convincing than the eucharist in Christian theology.[1]

The Politburo's overriding objective is to protect its own corporate identity and pretensions on the premise that its unity at any price, even more than its ability to solve problems in a manner consistent with its socialist ideals, is sufficient guarantee for the entire party to retain its hegemony. Were it to fail to do so, it argues, the party would lose its Marxist-Leninist historical mission. When victory came, it instantly became an anachronism and seriously counterproductive in a radically new context that demanded altogether different skills and responses. To a great extent, although certainly not wholly, Vietnam's profound crisis since 1975 is the product of the Politburo's dominating role in an environment which has wholly transcended its comprehension, organization, and abilities. Events have only reconfirmed the fundamental irrelevance of Leninist authoritarianism to peacetime conditions.

The precise differences among Politburo members are usually opaque, even though its leaders often employ superficial theoretical phrases to rationalize their positions. Many of the men who became the principal figures of the party after 1975 have been extremely astute at cultivating clientelist and regional alliances and loyal protégés, consolidating their authority with reciprocity or patronage systems – in effect, political machines – similar to those which politically ambitious men adopt in most nations. Some developed valuable talents during the long war, but few have possessed the aptitudes and resources essential for developing a peacetime economy and society on either a capitalist or socialist basis. Fewer yet have shown ability for creative thinking, instead allowing remarkably turgid and static phraseology to substitute for genuine analysis. The younger leadership generation beneath them that is now taking over power is comprised

overwhelmingly of managers and technocrats who think in functional problem-solving rather than political or ideological terms.
The party's secretary-general since 1991, Do Muoi, personifies this
trend. He is an opportunistic, intellectually banal figure who has
attempted to build a consensus among the various factions so that
the party only muddles from one immediate challenge to the next
rather than make difficult but urgent decisions. Vietnam's economic reforms have reflected the paralysis in the Politburo's
decision-making system and the confusion of men devoid both of
the deep knowledge and values essential for what is a monumental gamble with the very future of its founding socialist ideal.

The Politburo has accurately been described as a consensual,
collective leadership, but this does not so much mean that it
defines common policies on important issues as that it has learned
to live with its own differences without ever resorting to bloody
purges. To this extent, Vietnam has been totally unlike every other
Communist nation. It has on a few occasions dismissed members
who cannot for principled reasons accept compromises, which
usually consist of postponing crucial decisions so that the Politburo can coexist without a crisis in decision making. It generally
attains a consensus by agreeing to the lowest common denominator. It has therefore been highly effective in maintaining
its own unity, but at the price of repeatedly being indecisive
because it can neither agree nor – given its assumptions about the
way the nation should be organized – conceive of effective
solutions.

When the Politburo is irresolute or confused, or Hanoi simply
cannot implement a policy because of the logistical problems or
impotence inherent in its distance from the scene of action,
provincial and local authorities make the crucial decisions. This is
increasingly the case. There is a huge difference between the
party's centralizing pretensions and theory as opposed to the
reality, which makes the differences between conditions in the
various provinces often quite great. Given the way the war
encouraged local responsibility, it was hardly surprising that
much of the pressure for economic changes began in the south,
often as a result of unauthorized initiatives. At no time has a truly
comprehensive command economy ever been run from Hanoi,
and it never controlled the southern agricultural system after 1975
in anything like the manner it desired. After 1975 the provinces
were formally organized into regional bodies with greater auto-

nomy, and – as in China – they were assigned about half the seats on the central committee, often forming political blocs or alliances to advance their common local interests. Measures since then that decentralize power have been readily absorbed into this naturally receptive environment. *Doi moi* and the market line after 1986 greatly strengthened provincial authority in ways very similar to developments in China. After 1991 the Politburo attempted to retrieve many of these regional administrative powers but the provinces have retained a great deal of independence and often ignore Hanoi's orders or implement them to suit their own needs.[2] In essence, the Politburo often commands but its orders frequently go partly or wholly unheeded. Its real power has therefore eroded considerably, devolving to the party organizations. Authority has increasingly been decentralized, but not democratized.

Because the Vietnamese Politburo also comprises alliances and blocs, it is always essential to examine the relationship of its members to various interest groups, both in the center and regionally, since the provinces are now of crucial importance in influencing Hanoi's policies. The manner by which this political context influences economic ideas and strategies can be crucial. Leaders devoid of deep ideological commitments often evaluate proposals that have immense potential for harm in terms of how they advance coalitions built around ambition and tangible interests. It is also a situation where politics leads to patronage relationships to unify alliances, and this inevitably both encourages and protects corruption.

The party's rulers never accepted the logic that a mass mobilization party with millions of members must at some point create genuine popular participation and democracy within its ranks if it was to gain permanently its ranks' energy, devotion, and wisdom. Their contention that the Politburo was personally assuming the proletariat's role as the leading revolutionary class was conveniently self-serving, but as has occurred in all Leninist nations, it also eventually produced a growing gap between a tiny committee that claimed all power and the overwhelming majority of party members who were called upon to implement policies they never defined.

The logic of decentralized and disenfranchised mass movements must inevitably clash with all highly elitist, self-perpetuating parties, and it is a fundamental contradiction they ultimately cannot master. Given the inherent tension between Vietnam's physical and social realities and the party's centralizing assumptions, it could not devise a political structure capable of averting the dangers always inherent in its organizational form. For while the general population's unauthorized action may create risks to it, far more dangerous to the Politburo – and infinitely more difficult for it to control – is independence within the party's ranks itself. But such autonomy is precisely what Leninist elitism has produced everywhere, and Vietnam is only following in the wake of the East bloc and China, where all the parties discovered that their most formidable enemies were ultimately within their own ranks.

The enigma of human conduct

Vietnam's rulers since 1986 have enacted important legal and economic changes and simultaneously disparaged "voluntarism" (the appeal to the people to act selflessly for greater social goals) as sufficient to motivate economic behavior. In the past, however, "revolutionary morality" and social consciousness unquestionably were decisive to the Communists' successful struggle, for their capital was overwhelmingly human rather than material. Only immense personal sacrifices, and nothing less, produced victory. But a notion of individual conduct intended to promote larger social goals is scarcely a Marxist invention, and the avaricious but rational "economic man" so central to classical capitalist theory has never explained western economic development. Theories of motivation range from Max Weber's thesis of a Protestant concept of "grace" for those who accumulate capital to Joseph Schumpeter's visions of déclassé social elements who embark on crucial entrepreneurial risks to advance their class standing. Italy's preeminence in the European economy after the fourteenth century was closely linked to an intense notion of civic culture and philanthropy and produced the richest civilization Europe has ever seen. Variations of this sense of public responsibility also emerged in Holland in the seventeenth and eighteenth centuries. Ignoring both world and its own history, the party since 1986 has advocated a historically simplistic concept of acquisitiveness that also is embarrassingly inconsistent with its simultaneous advocacy of virtue.

Vietnam's leaders have worked themselves into an insoluble, incongruous, and inherently demoralizing position regarding the question of economic motivation and organization, the negative consequences of which are increasing rapidly. Socially oriented conduct, or "revolutionary morality," is the only possible barrier to the corruption that is today a grave epidemic corroding the morale of the party and society, and it is still evoked ritually but with little conviction. In the capitalist phase Vietnam has entered, the party has emphasized much more strongly the crudest possible classical laissez-faire concept of covetous individual motivations.[3] Rampant corruption has been the end result. In effect, unwilling and unable to discard entirely its socialist heritage, but increasingly committed to the capitalist road less for pragmatic reasons than because capitalism's core theses have convinced most of the Politburo that the doctrines it has held sacrosanct for over sixty years are now largely irrelevant, the party is maintaining two diametrically conflicting concepts of individual conduct at one and the same time. It has, therefore, created an impossible tension and a profound confusion regarding human behavior, one that is demoralizing its members and encouraging the worst aspects of its sanctioned acquisitive values.

Beginning no later than 1988, it became official doctrine that people have the right "to enrich themselves" in order to aid the nation, and since then the party has increasingly reiterated that it will "encourage everyone to get rich in a legitimate way."[4] But "to create favorable conditions for encouraging the people to amass wealth by honest means to become rich" has required the party to go one step further: to "combat egalitarianism."[5] Income must be distributed "to those who work and contribute more . . . in accordance with labor," and income equality must also be opposed "because such a move would destroy the motives behind production and business operations."[6] And although the magnitude of acceptable inequality is left vague, the party does not want it to go so far that "social conflicts will increase in intensity."[7] The state would unswervingly continue on this course, the party's 1994 conference reiterated; one of its solutions for poverty would be to "mobilize rich people" for "humanitarian and charitable activities."[8] "High esteem [for] those who invest . . . and who gain wealth honestly" is now official policy, and as Prime Minister

Vo Van Kiet put it at the end of 1995, "Any complexes or preconceptions against private economy should be eradicated. Businessmen should be encouraged. . . . "[9]

The majority of the Politburo's leaders now accept premises that no longer bear any relationship to the people's needs or the Communists' original ideas. Creating an equilibrium between high incentives and social peace, or the aggressive accumulation of wealth and no corruption, are inherently contradictory goals it cannot reconcile, and in the process the party's very raison d'être, if not its existence, is being challenged. That a Marxist-Leninist party should extol the virtues of becoming rich, while ignoring the historical origins and consequences of wealth, much less believe that charity is a solution for inequality, utterly devalues its founding ideology. By 1995 its new commitments had begun to undo all that it had accomplished in the economy and in transforming mass attitudes and values since 1945, and within a decade socialism has been gravely eroded except in the quixotic sense that the party believes that it still nominally rules the nation. A new class, emerging largely from within the party itself, has been behaving in ways that resemble closely the experiences of the Soviet bloc and China, and its policies are polarizing the nation. Functional power is passing increasingly to those in charge of specific economic sectors, either as state officials or managers, and to the provincial party apparatus. The party is disintegrating in terms of its ideological coherence and values, and the nation is decentralizing administratively as the Politburo in Hanoi becomes increasingly irrelevant.

The Communist party is in a profound crisis, and an altogether different society is being created.

The challenge of corruption

The men and few women who joined the party before August 1945 were rare idealists who could only anticipate great hardships, but the party's exponential growth after then opened it to a less select but nonetheless largely very devoted following – although a more educated intelligentsia controlled most key posts.[10] After 1954, party membership in the north provided access to power and privilege, and the motives of those who flocked to it were increasingly complex. Ambitious people join the party in power in every nation – whether socialist or capitalist – as a route to personal advancement, and the DRV also recruited what became an administrative class. With the passage of years, a growing portion of this elite was often quite apolitical. Their loyalties were principally to a system that rewarded them personally rather than to an ideology. Ho Chi Minh immediately recognized this problem, but such pliable members were indispensable insofar as the ruling committee's hegemony was concerned. Many had skills, and the older party leaders permitted them to become more important and, ultimately, powerful. The Politburo today regards technical qualifications as a precondition for leadership roles; it would prefer those who are both expert and Red, but expertise is now the preeminent, and often the only, criterion for advancement. As a result, it now admits publicly that party members in the state administration "account for a sizable percentage of those deviant and decadent cadres and civil servants. . . ."[11]

The south underwent a similar process, and the astonishingly heroic Communists who fought there facing incalculable dangers and hardships were overwhelmed after 1975 by a wave of *attentistes* and outright opportunists. At the end of the war they surfaced; I met a number of them when I was in the south during the final days of the war, and party officials confided to me their suspicions about their past roles and present motives. The idealistic Communists in the south always constituted a considerably smaller group than those who later joined it there or came from the north. By 1994, of the approximately 2.1 million party members, more than half had affiliated after 1975.[12] The vast majority live in the north and about nine-tenths are over thirty.

The party's social character and declining quality has increasingly disturbed its leaders, and by the mid-1980s they were publicly admitting "that most party cadres and members have committed numerous mistakes and shortcomings," including "theft . . . corruption . . . debauchery . . . [and] bureaucratism, arrogance, and bullying of the people."[13] They acknowledge that its faults have only grown greatly since then. Whatever the incessant encomiums on the value and purity of the party that are necessary to justify its monopoly of power, its own data reveal an organization that is rapidly decaying and imposing mounting hardships on the people. One official estimate in 1991 judged the party organization to be about 30 percent "strong," 10 percent "weak," and the remainder implicitly somewhere in between.[14]

Of the rural party members, or nearly one-half of the organization, in 1991 "only 20–25 percent . . . brought into play their exemplary vanguard role."[15] One senior leader in 1990 thought that 30–40 percent of the party should be purged.[16] By 1995 the situation had become even worse, and although reports on membership quality differed greatly according to what regional organizations were ready to confess, in Ho Chi Minh City "The overall condition of party members was poor."[17] No matter what the figures, virtually all accounts admitted that their lack of initiative and lassitude was pervasive.

Party cells now meet much less frequently, and the party's political report to the June 1996 congress admitted that "grass-roots party organizations are weak in many localities. Some are even paralyzed."[18] Leaders often detail the innumerable weaknesses among the membership: "many cadres and party members are losing their revolutionary ideals and are becoming alienated. . . ."[19] The leading official daily newspaper in the spring of 1996 admitted that the public overwhelmingly believed that "bureaucracy, corruption and smuggling . . . are spreading as a national catastrophe."[20] This decay has far outrun measures to correct it. The party ranks' allegedly elite quality was always a crucial justification for its authority. But while this illusion of a select membership has been openly and thoroughly shattered in the minds of both its leaders and the people, the party continues to rule; it has lost its justificatory myth, without which it ultimately cannot survive. Indeed, its corrupt members' real power in the day-to-day world has grown consistently.

Whatever the monumental implications of a party comprised of roughly two-thirds poor or indifferent people called upon to administer the nation, the party's leaders have publicly and consistently deplored the members' increasing deterioration in the strongest possible terms; but they ultimately have no one but themselves to blame for the fact. They have been unable to reconcile the inherent tension between absolute discipline and high morale in a way that prevents the immense risks of growing organizational rot. Senior party leaders have admitted for some years that cadres are increasingly cynical careerists "generally not up to duties or requirements" who "act in an irresponsible manner," if they are not "authoritarian." Worse yet, many are often "engaging in economic activities for their families" as a new and oppressive rural elite.[21] Do Muoi complained in February 1995:

> A large number of cadres, from the central down to the grassroots level have distanced themselves from the masses while adopting an aristocratic and coercive attitude toward the people. . . . They violate the people's rights and interests . . . engage in corruption and embezzlement . . . demand bribes, and amass wealth illegally.[22]

"Revolutionary mandarins" is how Prime Minister Vo Van Kiet, the leading exponent of the "market" line and whose wife has been publicly implicated in massive corruption, described them in early 1995.[23] Precisely because their control of the party organization in a town or region determines the extent to which local leaders can enrich themselves and their clients, intraparty disputes for the control over bureaucracies and territory have grown significantly, and internal party struggles increasingly focus on administrative jurisdictions that involve control over power and wealth rather than political or ideological issues. Since loyalty in politics provides protection, such machines routinely shield their members from corruption charges.[24]

By the 1990s, the magnitude of the party members' corruption and fraud had eroded a great deal of the immense credibility that the Communists had gained before 1975. Every senior party leader publicly recognizes this dilemma but none has proposed an effective solution to it.

Corruption in the party was minor before 1975, above all among those in crucial positions of responsibility or danger. Obviously, some of those who joined the northern party after 1954 exploited various advantages, but it was never substantial or very noticeable. But there was always major institutionalized favoritism after 1954 in the form of education at home and in the East bloc (and often protection from dangerous wartime assignments) that was given to the children of more important party members. Indeed, it was especially their children's welfare that later caused many party members to waver from what was once deemed revolutionary morality and honesty, and it is these privileged descendants who are most likely – as in the USSR and China – to abandon socialism and rule whatever hybrid society follows in its wake.

The major cause of the cadres' deterioration was the inflation during the 1980s and the inordinately low salaries for civil servants and government officials that was imposed at that time on the advice of the IMF; many, as a consequence, were seriously demoralized. The real income of civil servants dropped by about two-thirds from 1985 to 1991, by which point cadres were compelled to choose between corruption, leaving the state sector, or going hungry, and many chose or were compelled to cheat.[25] In 1993 most civil servants earned between $15 and $20 a month, less than half the wages for skilled workers, and their real incomes have continued to deteriorate since then.[26]

The countless forms this corruption takes are routinely and openly described in the Vietnamese press: "extravagant spending seen in massive offices ... and luxury cars." Demanding bribes for "oiling the road of [licensing] procedures, up to 20, 30, or in certain cases even 50 percent of the project costs ... misappropriated tax money," and the like.[27] In one comprehensive audit of ninety-nine state-controlled agencies in Ho Chi Minh City in 1993, "most of these establishments had violated the state regulations."[28] Outright corruption is pervasive.

Since commercializing influence also borders on corruption, even the party central committee's own role became questionable when it began to operate its own enterprises. The largest exposed fraud scandal as of mid-1996 involved a party-owned company. In 1995 it created a branch that is negotiating participation in at least one very large international investment fund. Since it has neither capital nor expertise in the normal commercial sense, all it can do is monetize its ability as the ruling party to offer foreign capitalists lucrative opportunities – which means selling influence.[29] The distinction with corruption is largely semantic, and what is clear is that it is itself not the ideal model of probity.

While Politburo members repeatedly deplore the members' laxity in their public jeremiads, the irony of this astonishing exposure of the party's disastrous collapse of ethics is that the very men who excoriate it are responsible for its existence. Worse yet, they have neither the ability nor desire to act decisively to reverse the profound malaise. There is no question that many who joined the party were from the inception opportunists susceptible to corruption, but a very substantial proportion of the culprits were compelled to behave according to those acquisitive "market" principles the Politburo has idealized. Corruption is the consequence of the fundamental contradictions inherent in the Politburo's daringly utopian synthesis of capitalism and socialism, and it again confirms the crucial role of elan rather than growth rates for balanced, long-term development.

The party's leaders had few illusions by 1990 concerning the impact of their economic policies on the organization's structure itself, much less on the remainder of the nation. Even the army, which resisted the infection longer than any other major institution, by 1993 was becoming involved in smuggling and corruption, if only because it had trucks, access to borders, and its officers' inadequate salaries created irresistible temptations. As Nguyen Van Linh, who as much as anyone helped frame the new line, put it in May 1993:

> bureaucratism, corruption, and bribery ... have reached a serious level without any sign of abating. Not a small number of people, including leading cadres in charge of high-level leadership and management apparatuses, have taken advantage of loopholes in mechanisms and policies to misappropriate public funds, accept bribes, and seek personal gains in an illegal manner.... Corruption, smuggling, and bribery have reached such a widespread and alarming proportion that many people regard them as a national disaster.[30]

"If the ills of corruption and smuggling continue to prevail," Politburo member Le Phuoc Tho warned in July 1994, "we will lose our cadres and the people's trust in the party's leadership."[31] A Hong Kong economic risk consultancy in early 1996 ranked Vietnam as one of Asia's three most corrupt nations. What remains is a party whose authority depends less and less on its moral standing as leader of a triumphant war than on its access to privilege and control of power.[32]

While it is impossible to estimate the direct, much less the indirect, cost of corruption in its numerous forms, it is especially significant in smuggling and in the disposal of state-owned land. Smuggling, which involves many state employees, had by 1990 reached massive dimensions – an "epidemic," in the words of one official source – and it is far more serious today.[33] Smuggled imports in 1995 were estimated at $1.8 billion, compared to $6.5 billion in legal imports from the entire world. Roughly one-quarter of Vietnam's imports – especially the half-million or more motorcycles that were illegally brought in after 1991 – are not taxed and this has seriously reduced the market for Vietnam's nascent industry, in addition to reducing its control over foreign exchange.[34] The state admits that the responsible law-enforcement agencies have failed abysmally, and that "some leading cadres of anti-smuggling organs are also smugglers themselves."[35]

Violations involving state-owned land are probably even more serious. Land is capital which can be sold or serve as collateral for loans, and by 1994 "extremely serious violations of the Land Law" were widespread.[36] Forty thousand known infractions had occurred by mid-1995, and they were common in all the large cities and especially in the countryside, where about 4 million hectares of agricultural land are being transferred to private owners, thereby making illegal confiscations common. Enormous sums have been gained through illegal land transfers, and in numerous areas "many cadres, including leading cadres at the primary level, have allocated and sold land in order to share tens of billions of dong . . . the illegal sale of land in Ho Chi Minh City has been going on for many years. . . ."[37] Many corrupt officials "have enriched themselves overnight."[38]

Since the population is primarily rural, these massive land abuses have been far more visible and have profoundly alienated the peasantry. The potential consequences of this reality cannot be overestimated, and while the party's leaders are supremely conscious of it, they have neither the means nor the will to reverse it. Because the public has no reliable way of protesting against corruption without fear of reprisals, the number of anonymous complaints against cadres has been increasing substantially, and where investigations have occurred, up to 90 percent of the accusations have been vindicated in whole or part.[39] Indeed, most major corruption cases that have surfaced are the result of public or mass media denunciations; the party has been unable to police itself, and most malefactors are party members. By 1995, Nguyen Van Linh and at least one Politburo member publicly conceded that since those responsible for controlling corruption were among those most guilty of it, people from outside the party should also be assigned to policing functions – in effect, to watch party members. Linh by then had become one of the strongest critics of the consequences of the *doi moi* strategy that he, more than anyone, initiated.[40]

The difficulty is that very few party members who are accused are ever convicted. The chances of their being prosecuted and then penalized by either the courts or the party are extremely small, and they decline with the individual's power and connections. Because corruption often originates with urban and provincial party alliances or factions that work on a reciprocal, clientelist basis, and is therefore virtually legitimized, "a number of influential cadres also tried to protect corrupt elements and bribe takers."[41] It supplies cohesion where ideological and political issues long since ceased to have any influence. Meanwhile, the party leaders publicly admit: "The quality of the cadres is declining, and corruption among cadres is increasing."[42] Because of this parasitical constituency, the Politburo can proclaim whatever policies it desires, but a growing number of members behave as they wish, so that the distance between its decisions and their implementation is growing rapidly. Ironically, to the extent that the members neither contest nor obey them, the leaders' nominal authoritarianism has decisive, perhaps fatal, limits. "Once a person has spoken about an issue," Nguyen Duc Binh, chief theoretician and a Politburo member, complained in June 1992, "others seem to be unable to say anything else."[43] In early 1994, ranking Politburo member Vu Oanh accurately assessed the situation which its hierarchical policies had created:

> Lower level cadres do not dare tell the truth to higher cadres. . . . The principle of democratic centralism, which is the party's vitality, has not been maintained. The practice of bureaucracy and authoritarianism has existed together with the devils of indiscipline, sectionalism, and clannishness.[44]

No one is more aware of the precarious condition of the party as a ruling institution than those responsible for leading it over twenty years since the war ended.

Corruption is becoming the scourge of the party and therefore the nation, depriving the leaders of the obedience they covet and making it impossible to attain *any* type of rational, durable economy. It is now systemic and it has made access to political and state power, not creative economic entrepreneurship, the principal determinant of who becomes rich and, above all, how they do so. It is the party itself, insulated from real reform but desperately in need of it, that has become the primary inhibition to the attainment of either socialism *or* something akin to the theoretical capitalist model.

The crisis in morale

In a context of urging people to enrich themselves but unable to control how they do so, the Communist party is undergoing a profound crisis in morale and values which has trapped it in its own irreconcilable contradictions and sapped it of self-confidence. In a profound sense, the Politburo is gradually becoming ir- relevant as countless individuals and groups within the party pursue their own self-interest with scant regard for its authority. It has no one but itself to blame for this impasse, because it is confused on fundamental economic and social policies and in- capable of reconciling its internal differences.

The Politburo, and through it the party itself, has lost much of its credibility among the people, who no longer believe, according to opinion surveys released by the government itself, "that lead- ing and management cadres from the central down to the grass- roots levels set examples for others with regard to fighting corruption. . . ."[45] The wives of at least two present or former leading Politburo members have been publicly identified as extremely corrupt, and in early 1996 a group of war veterans excoriated high party leaders for their hypocrisy in attacking alleged public decadence. Party writers admit that the massive resurgence since 1990 of superstition, Buddhism, and Christianity, especially among young people, is due to the disorientation its own policies and behavior have engendered.

The attack on foreign "social evils and cultural poisons" mounted at the beginning of 1996 (mainly against the advertising of imported goods) only intensified mass cynicism because the state itself has courted foreign investment and the campaign was neither effective nor long lasting. Hedonism and pleasure-seeking among younger people in the cities – night clubs, rock music, Coke and fast motorcycles and all of the symptoms of alienation and confusion – are rampant. Since such conspicuous consumption costs far more than workers and peasants can afford, it has from its inception always been especially pronounced among the chil- dren of party members, particularly in the north, and it only heightens the tensions between the masses and the privileged elite. This paradox is also one of the reasons very little is done to suppress what is a continuous reminder of the party's failure to create an appealing culture for its own children. Indeed, a growing number of party members are themselves a part of this demimonde – they have money and spend it openly, and they no longer take the party's pretensions seriously.

On one hand the party has a Leninist commitment to authoritarian discipline – "unity and single-mindedness within the party and between the party and people" is the most recent phrasing of it – which it openly admits is not effective in countless ways; on the other is its ostensible adherence to "a state of the people, by the people, and for the people" and "to broaden[ing] democracy in society in general and within the party in particular."[46] But not only do the people not rule in any meaningful way but the Politburo itself is increasingly unable to impose its own ostensible authority. The Politburo claims mastery not because of the legitimacy earned from its present leadership roles but simply because it is at the top of the hierarchy and it possesses the force to remain there. It is surviving on myths and illusions, and reality is increasingly bypassing it. It is in an unenviable, precarious position.

The party is losing the loyalty of its own members as well as the respect of a people that once sacrificed heroically for common national goals. It is increasingly being endangered because of a policy that has produced a new economic elite comprised to a large extent of the corrupt ranks of the party itself – a plutocracy that can also employ its political power cynically to defend its economic privilege in the name of pretentious but now irrelevant rhetoric. How and when this loss of faith and malaise will affect the party's very existence cannot be predicted, but there are few examples in modern history of societies that have undergone such a profoundly disorienting transformation in the past and survived intact.

Two major dangers confront the Politburo today. The most obvious is from its weak members. In light of the Soviet and East bloc experience, it cannot be certain which of its members or senior party leaders will stand with it in case the party's hegemony is threatened – and who will betray it. It cannot, without being blind to the fate of its "fraternal" parties elsewhere, in any way be confident that treachery is not close at hand.

On the other hand, there also exists a latent but growing danger from those members who remain deeply committed to socialist goals and values and who increasingly feel deceived that a self-perpetuating, largely irresponsible and incompetent handful of men is gravely endangering a cause to which they have devoted their entire lives. Whatever may be wrong with a large portion of the party, a great many of the Communists I met over thirty years were remarkable and astonishingly brave people, incapable of playing lightly with their deepest ethical commitments. The best were strong, devoted to socialism defined broadly as a moral and equitable system, and very serious. I have always respected them greatly both as genuine radicals and as human beings in the finest, all-too-rare sense of that term. There are also countless tough and brave men and women who made a revolution; they are increasingly distressed with the nation's direction. The Politburo takes this considerable element's traditional loyalty for granted, and therefore abuses it. They remain a substantial share of the party, and they have been relatively – but certainly not wholly – passive compared to the corrupt and lazy members. They cannot be discounted, and at some point, probably too late in this tragic drama, they may increasingly be tempted to act. Indeed, by 1995 the serious possibility of an open split within the party – the first since it was founded – began to emerge. I discuss this prospect in Chapter 6, but suffice it to say, the party's moral impasse has intensified greatly the tension within its own ranks, producing growing instability.

BUREAUCRACY VERSUS THE MASS LINE

Faced with a profound crisis in morale and within the organization, the Communist party's leaders have been unable to confront their dilemmas. The Politburo not only repeatedly acknowledges these problems but it continues to revel in minute accounts of them as if self-criticism alone is sufficient to resolve the challenge and win public toleration for policies that only perpetuate the grave malady. After all, the proclaimed aim of the Revolution was not to keep a tiny coterie in power but to build an equitable, just society. Yet the Politburo has turned the perpetuation of its own hegemony into the overriding goal of the political system – thereby endangering the very future of the Revolution and those larger objectives that justified its existence.

References to the evils of "bureaucratism, authoritarianism, and the practice of distancing oneself from the people" have suffused the party's declarations over the past decade, but became especially profuse after it formally embarked on its renovation policy in December 1986.[47] *Doi moi* closely paralleled Gorbachev's *perestroika* reforms in the USSR, and while it implied the desire to make broad changes in politics as well as economics, politically it remained an ambiguous expression of intentions rather than a blueprint committing the Politburo to definite changes. Only its economic dimensions have continued without respite. Theoretically, it evolved out of the ostensible party tenet that there could be no struggle against bureaucracy without "democratization," and to deny the latter would only perpetuate those organizational evils against which Ho Chi Minh and his followers always inveighed.[48] But since 1986, the leaders' statements have repeatedly confirmed the growing existence of organizational obstacles to their control of the economy, especially in the provinces. To cope with all the countless difficulties that its wayward members, bureaucrats, and local parties increasingly present to the Politburo, it quixotically aspires to mobilize the masses in a controlled manner intended, ironically, only to counteract the erosion of its own authoritarian hegemony.

There has always been uncomfortable tension between the Communists' theory of a highly centralized, elitist organization and the reality of a huge party based on masses who were, at best, ideologically less developed. Their practice was wholly authoritarian when possible, but this became increasingly difficult to implement as the party grew in size and space. The mass party, by definition, cannot conform to the Leninist model, and open recruitment was precisely what Lenin opposed when he first articulated Bolshevik theory. But since success was wholly dependent on mobilizing virtually everyone willing to join, the Vietnamese, like all other Communist parties, compromised on fundamental doctrine. This practice was essentially subversive of Bolshevism, but the pure party, as Lenin defined it, has never existed anywhere that Communists have come to power. Ho Chi Minh's powerful influence discouraged ideological rigidity in favor of pragmatism.

Balancing elite theory against its mass reality always produced an unavoidable dilemma for the Vietnamese party. This enigma, and the sincerity that motivated it, has always made the Vietnamese the least doctrinaire and most attractive of all the successful Communist parties. Ho Chi Minh made attacks on "bureaucratism" integral to the party's ideas, and he advocated the "mass line" as an antidote to controls inherent in Leninist theory in the

hope that it could create a distinctive working-style transcending
Bolshevik authoritarianism. The tension between these two con-
ceptions was in reality a struggle between dictatorial and democratic impulses, and the party at crucial junctures was compelled
to concede to the people's desires as the only means of both
harnessing their enthusiasm and organizing an inherently diffuse
war effort functionally in a decentralized nation. Had the party's
leaders not acceded to the population's priorities at various
decisive points, or mass organizations not often supplanted a
disciplined party's roles, the Communists would have lost the
war. While the mass line reflected necessity in most cases, it has
always had a certain autonomous logic and vitality of its own. It
was always, in a fashion, the subversive democratic seed within
Communist doctrine.

The problem is that the elitist intelligentsia who have ruled the
party since its formation have in the final analysis been unable and
unwilling to reconcile the diametrically different organizational
implications of an antibureaucratic, mass line with their absolute
control of power, largely because they deem themselves to be in
some transcendent sense an elect – the "proletariat's" historical
agent, according to erstwhile Leninist laws. So long as there was
a war and the party leaders could justify their hegemony for
reasons of military necessity, the people on the whole accepted
and supported Communist rule. But the ultimate logic of the mass
line is real democracy, and with the present grave crisis in the
party's morale and direction, its leaders have explicitly conceded
that it is essential to motivate the people again in the hope of
renewing and legitimizing the constituted order – not so much for
the purposes of democracy itself, however, as to prevent Vietnam
from going the way of the East bloc nations. This effort to reconcile
such inherently conflicting impulses and objectives reflects its
absolute ideological confusion.

The precondition for resolving the impasse eroding the party
and society is to reestablish its credibility with the majority who
are and will remain poor, and to implement those larger social
goals that it professes to believe in. If it does not, it will increasingly lose even more authority and, in one manner or another, real
power. Meanwhile, the Politburo's single most pressing problem
today is with the party membership and organization, especially
in the provinces, which it seeks to command but that increasingly

ignores it. The leaders' fundamental challenge is that both the
people and the party's own members have lost confidence in them.

After years of assigning the so-called mass organizations a ceremonial, perfunctory role, the party after 1987 began to increase its
emphasis on the "mass line." But at the same time it has suppressed genuinely independent expressions of mass opinion,
especially among army veterans, intellectuals, and, to a lesser
extent, workers. Given the rapid dissolution of all the structures
and values that galvanized the people after 1945, and its present
dismissal of those motives that convinced people to make immense sacrifices during the nation's most trying times as "voluntarism," the party now must animate the masses as an antidote to
the rampant cynicism and disillusion that has necessarily accom-
panied its market philosophy. Compelled to call again upon the
"masses," whose attitudes and conduct will ultimately determine
the fate of the entire Vietnamese experience with the party, its
leaders must do so in a profoundly altered context. Since its
capitalist economic policies damage especially the welfare of
precisely those constituencies that have supported the Communists most in the past, the decisive question is whether the party
can now successfully employ purely organizational and rhetorical
exhortations that are devoid of class interests. While the two
dramatically different visions of how and why people should
behave are irreconcilable, they reflect two very different tendencies that have emerged for the first time in its history within the
Politburo itself – one held by a few members, the other by the large
majority.

During the first several years of *doi moi*, the party's mass line
was fairly strong, even unequivocal, in calling for genuinely
"independent and self-managing organizations" – in the words
of the party's draft platform in December 1990 – which took the
initiative and acted creatively, as indeed lower party cadres were
at the same time also urged to do despite senior-level com-
mandism.[49] But the party's leaders sought to balance their desire
to use the mass organizations as convenient, tightly controlled
conduits for its policies against their fear of "alienation from the
masses."[50] High-level disagreements persisted on how much
genuine freedom should be allowed the public, and these im-
pinged on the whole question of political and human rights as

well. During 1990 the leaders' growing fears of a Vietnamese equivalent of Poland's Solidarity movement or China's Tiananmen Square, and the acknowledged failure of its efforts to renovate decrepit mass groups that had become sinecures for some older cadres, caused most of them to back away from real changes.[51] The mass-line concept, if carried to its logical conclusion, contains the potential for challenging the party's claim to mastery. In its extreme form, it leads to democracy – or "peaceful evolution" in its demonology.

Notwithstanding the more democratic notions of Nguyen Duc Binh, number three Politburo member and head of the party school, the consensus in party directives from 1990 through 1994 was to reassert much more rigorously the party's need to dominate the mass fronts while galvanizing them for purely instrumental reasons; far less was said about their independent functions. But since then it has consistently acknowledged its failure to renew the masses' devotion or to regain their enormous resources, enthusiasm, and energy. The grave dilemma facing it was that the Politburo was also increasingly losing control of the party, and the senior Politburo member in charge of mass work, Vu Oanh, made a series of radical proposals which directly challenged the party's centralist organizational doctrine. Nothing remotely like it had ever occurred, and it reflected the gravity of the party's crisis.

Were it not for the fact these efforts in the past have all foundered because of the party's refusal to relinquish a monopoly of power, the mass line campaign's objectives would seem cynical and manipulative. The problem is that it has never confronted a crisis within its own membership of such magnitude, and Oanh defied all taboos. "A mechanism must be built so that the people can participate in criticizing the party organizations and party members," as he expressed it in August 1995, "and participate in building the leading organizations and formulating the political tasks of the primary-level party organization. . . . Democracy must be expanded even more with respect to politics, the economy, and society. . . . "[52] The party, in effect, had to be controlled from outside its own ranks.

The following month Oanh went one giant step further and publicly committed rank heresy; he was specific in ways that were unprecedented. Indeed, his proposals would be considered too radical in most nominally democratic states:

For the people's right to mastery to be fully implemented, first of all we must institutionalize democracy in all the three aspects: *representative* democracy, *direct* democracy, and *self-management* democracy at the grass-roots level. Prior to their promulgation, draft laws and policies bearing on the people's interest and obligations should be subjected to public comment. The administration must be directly led by the people, and mass organizations must be built by the people. Autocracy, arbitrariness, perfunctoriness, and imposition of policy by the upper levels on the lower levels, which would result in superficial democracy, must be overcome. The people must be motivated to participate in building the party and reforming the national administrative system. A mechanism should be institutionalized at an early date to periodically solicit public comment on party cadres and elected officials.[53]

Oanh proposed a radical alternative to the party's political malaise, although he said nothing about crucial economic questions. Nguyen Van Linh at the same time publicly took an even stronger position in favor of a grass roots movement "to help the party correct, rectify, and overcome its shortcomings."[54]

By this time it was obvious that a very significant portion of the party's membership was beyond redemption, and in the discussion in the months leading up to the June 1996 party congress many leaders stressed the mass line's importance in saving the party from the logic of its internal organizational contradictions. There were unrelenting public attacks by older party members on "corruption and bureaucracy," and the Politburo knew that it had to appear to be in favor of encouraging this approach.[55] There were even references to the Fatherland Front, the official mass organization, verifying that party committees investigating corruption were not themselves dishonest. The mass organizations' roles, the party congress resolved, should involve the "control" of the "major decisions and policies of the party and state," although how this was to occur was conspicuously vague.[56]

The real question was whether the Politburo would abandon its traditional policy of favoring only tightly controlled mass work. Vu Oanh himself slightly softened his position just before the June meeting, but while its political report to the congress contained the spirit and rhetoric of his proposals, with fulsome references to "self-management groups" and "structures for the people to exercise their right of mastery through representatives elected by the people's organs or mass organizations," it left no doubt whatsoever that the party would stay firmly in command.[57] At its core, its position remains deeply ambiguous. To make the point unmistakably clear, Vu Oanh was dropped from both the Politburo and the central committee.

The Politburo as a body regards the party organizations at the local and provincial levels rather than its own role as a principal source of the nation's problems. In essence, however sincere its most ardent advocates, its populist critique of its members and professions of democracy are entirely manipulative. Essentially, it aspires to empower itself, not the masses. But that the mass line is repeatedly evoked reveals both a genuine, residual core commitment to the people among a minority of top leaders which, despite the pathetic manner in which it has been articulated, cannot be dismissed entirely. More important, it confirms the repeated failures of the party's earlier efforts to transform the passive role that the public plays in society – and the profound limits inherent in its Leninist commitments.

While it can be interpreted in very different ways, the mass line under the right circumstances could greatly undermine the party's organizational centralism even while allowing it to play a role in the process. It is fundamentally antithetical to Leninist doctrine, and its persistence this long reflects how diluted the party's original orthodoxy has become – this, by itself, is encouraging. So long as the notion is tolerated, there remains an ideological basis for challenging authoritarianism. The Communist party cannot afford casually to forsake the "mass line" because the illusion that the party can redeem itself and retain its original socialist commitment will then disappear, and total disillusion will prevail. Even more dangerous to it, it will abandon the only means it has left for reversing the organizational malaise into which it has fallen.

Whatever it chooses to do, the party cannot much longer evade decisions that will profoundly affect its very future. It must take its chances with democratic institutions or by default accept the continuing irresistible transformation of the party into provincial fiefdoms and a corrupt organization that makes a total mockery of its revolution. As even a few Politburo members concede, it is too late for the party to cure itself. If it cannot trust the masses in the future as it did in the past, socialism will become a myth justifying an exploitative society.

The Politburo's greatest challenge – and danger – is that it cannot predict the ultimate consequence of either its action or its passivity, and it cannot escape one or the other. For better or worse, Vietnam, like all the Communist nations, will undergo a very profound change in the near future.

Chapter 4

Land and the crisis of rural society

By far the single most important consequence of the Communist party's new policy has been seen in agriculture, which absorbed nearly three-quarters of the work force in 1991 and accounted for about two-fifths of the national income. Whatever their productive efficiency, cooperatives after 1959 created a form of social insurance and security that was adapted perfectly to the needs of soldiers at war, their families, and veterans. Well over five million veterans and retired cadres in the late 1980s, plus over a million soldiers, benefited from the existing cooperative structure. Their interests, and the fact that the army and coops have always reinforced each other, is a principal reason for the military's strong opposition to so-called reforms. Moreover, many peasants in the poorer central and northern regions supported cooperatives because they insulated them from the innumerable hardships inherent in agriculture, creating a social safety net that provided health and education services that were the best in Southeast Asia. Agriculture may not have been optimally efficient in terms of output, though it developed very significantly by any criterion, but socially coops produced a cohesive rural system adjusted to the needs of the majority of the peasantry for two decades.

Peace immediately altered much of the utility of what was, in effect, a wartime as well as a socialist agricultural structure, and after 1975 most of the peasants in the Mekong Delta, the area with the greatest potential, resisted the collectivization initiated in April 1978. Numerous peasants, in any case, also had extensive short-term land contracts while belonging to cooperatives, and gaining their enthusiasm was considered crucial to achieving greater output. Elsewhere, many households informally circumvented the legal land structure in various ways, and by 1981 these were increasingly accepted; but the cooperatives in the north and center still performed crucial functions. In 1988, in by far the single most important phase of *doi moi*, the party enacted a series of land laws allocating land to farmers for variable periods of ten to nineteen years and favoring those who were most productive. Because of strong opposition to it, these reforms at their inception were quite ambiguous.

The new measures recognized the rights of inheritance and transfer, but only in 1993 were the reforms further clarified to fully institutionalize private agriculture. By that time, six of the nearly eight million hectares of cropland were in one way or another already under or targeted for direct household control. The 1993 law initially limits individual households to three hectares and the tenure to twenty years for annual crops and fifty years for long-term crops, but it permits land to be traded, leased, inherited, and mortgaged, thereby allowing it – as the World Bank advised – to be concentrated into fewer and fewer hands. But the fact that the laws and rules for managing land affairs remained obscure and inadequate opened the door to administratively arbitrary – and corrupt – practices. Although the government will not admit it outright, it has created a land market. Even at its June 1996 congress the party wistfully claimed that whatever the past concessions, land was ultimately the property of the state.

The party radically transformed the entire land system, which is tantamount to most of the nation's social structure, in a swift, virtually frivolous manner, the consequences of which could be enormous. To make any error whatsoever in this domain must affect the welfare of a large part of the peasantry – and it could prove decisive to the party's very future. It assumed, as with the nonfarm sector, that if the "market" decided agriculture's future then prosperity was inevitable and the vast change would be relatively simple. It went much further toward imposing a true unregulated market in agriculture than in industry, leaving an immense institutional void in all those domains in which the cooperatives had for decades played a decisive role. No effort whatsoever was made to retain the socialist system's positive functions. It failed to enact legislation or rules covering virtually every other important aspect of rural society: credit, maintenance of the existing irrigation and service infrastructure, rural labor standards, the health and education systems the coops had funded, and much else. Nothing was done to protect the poorer peasants, which is to say the majority of them, from the profound change that was occurring. The party correctly believed that the more prosperous and productive peasants would grow much more rice, but also that a system conforming to the putative laws of the market would create a new, more natural social equilibrium. The focus was on increasing output, whatever the cost. The very social class that had done the most to make the Communist victory possible was abandoned to a competitive world very much like that idealized by laissez-faire economists over a century ago. There was no compromise between total control and total freedom, and the party was oblivious to the social consequences of its decision.

About 4 million hectares of land were scheduled for reallocation after 1988, most of which has been disposed of, initiating a protracted and still incomplete transformation that has profoundly shattered the entire established rural social and political order in an infinite number of ways, ranging from which family within a village received specific, well-tended plots rather than marginal land, to boundaries and jurisdictions between villages which had never been contested before but which now became of utmost importance to the prosperity of a community. The basic structure of what had once been the large majority of the nation's relatively stable, organized universe was now placed under severe stress and profoundly traumatized – especially in the northern Red River Delta and along the central coast. It was entirely predictable that the reallocation of land would necessarily affect rural social peace fundamentally for a very long time, creating incalculable risks. This was all the more likely because the sudden decline of the coops no longer insulated the peasants from the hard realities of farming in the merciless new order.[1]

The cooperatives after 1988 were in principle still allocated a vague responsibility for services such as credit, marketing, and irrigation, but in practice they almost immediately reduced greatly their former roles and began to disintegrate. There is no doubt that the large majority of the peasants wanted major changes in the existing system, but subsequent events showed that they also both desired and required many of its crucial functions; this was particularly true among poorer peasants in the less-productive regions in the center and north who have always been economically marginal, had few illusions about becoming rich, and were now, like peasants everywhere, exposed to all the perils inherent in agriculture. Although the pattern varied substantially among and within regions, as the coops dissolved the rural party organizations also began to weaken greatly. Within a few years, as the central committee admitted much later, many coops disappeared or "exist[ed] only in name." In a significant number of villages, even the local parties "have not been operational"; some continued only because the cadres could exploit their power. The credit coops in others "collapsed," and the dreaded usury system from the French era quickly returned. With it came the threat of a land system that resembled that under the French.[2]

The Politburo failed to comprehend that the problem of land in an agrarian nation is not simply a matter of measuring rice output statistics, as the World Bank had convinced it, but principally of attaining a balanced development that could assure both stability in the nation's fundamental social system and create the structural preconditions for sustained growth over the long run. By remaining oblivious to the human and therefore political risks of its policies, it confirmed its inability to perform the vast responsibilities it sought to monopolize. Land, in all of its dimensions, from the organization of rural society to the manner of its exploitation, is likely to become the party's biggest failure. Even if it were its only challenge, its very future may be determined by the land problem alone, especially if one considers its moral and political implications to the party's legitimacy among the masses.

THE PEASANTS BEGIN TO STIR

The precise magnitude of peasant discontent since 1988 cannot be estimated, but it is far more significant than anything the party has confronted since the 1955–6 land reform conflicts that profoundly traumatized the north. Above all, the turmoil has lasted much longer and there is no resolution in sight because the party inadvertently reintroduced class struggle into the countryside. From its inception, the land redistribution was marred by conflict, ambiguity, and corruption. Cadres in many villages immediately began to distribute the best land to their families and relatives, and abuse was rife. The party, with ironic justice, is now trapped by the very egalitarian ideology it preached for generations and has now abandoned; for an indeterminate but unquestionably important share of the people still believe in it.

The party's problem is that many who fought and suffered during the war are now locked in disputes over land, which it terms "hot spots," including a significant number of party members in villages. Every conceivable grievance has arisen, and they have included petitions and bitter arguments between neighbors; but "there have even been cases in which militia and self-defense forces have been mobilized to attack people," and clashes between official armed security forces. "A large number of people" have participated in "hot spots that have arisen spontaneously for a variety of reasons."[3] Arms are not often used, but they too have been reported. Peasants who received poor or too little land sometimes illegally occupied fallow land. As the official radio in July 1988 reported one incident, "the authorities mobilized the armed forces to tear down these peasants' houses and open fire to threaten them, thus causing conflict between poor peasants, families of the sick, fallen combatants, and the village authorities."[4] The entire transformation of the land system began very badly – and it only got worse.

About 200,000 written complaints on land-use rights were submitted in writing from 1988 to mid-1990 alone. Unprecedentedly large crowd scenes, with threats or actual acts of violence, have occurred. By itself, this is astonishing. One account of 120 acute hot spots in Thanh Hoa province between 1988 and 1992 alone, if projected nationally, suggests that there were at least 2,600 during that period, and perhaps many more. Forty percent were categorized as "smoldering," 49 percent "tense," and 11 percent "very fierce," the latter involving violence.[5] Over half the disputes were over arable land; 19 percent of the conflicts were between the masses and the cadres. A third of the conflicts were between people in one village and outsiders, seriously disrupting social cohesion within regions in unprecedented ways. Only a quarter of them were fully resolved permanently within this time, but a third remained contested, and 40 percent were stabilized. In effect, the revolution in land relations has produced continuous turmoil and strife in the rural society, above all in the north and center of the country.

There have been an increasing number of press accounts since 1994 of "land and market disputes" that were threatening "to cause social explosions."[6] By 1995, the party admitted publicly, these problems were "becoming more and more complex and serious," with "strikes, market walkouts, demonstrations displaying signs and slogans, road blockages to intercept government vehicles, and so on." Nothing like it had ever occurred previously, but now the people's complaints, as party journals admitted, were mostly "truthful and constructive," and it either could not or would not stop them.[7] "Land disputes are common," as two Vietnamese experts state, since they determine who will gain most, or least, in the new order.[8] "Unless these are controlled," senior leaders admitted at the end of 1995, "they will lead to danger and social turmoil."[9] Most ominous is the fact that these conflicts are producing natural leaders, and the party alleges that some have created illegal organizations which claim, in effect, that the Communists have abandoned their populist commitment. If a clandestine movement for social justice ever emerges among the peasants – and that it may is only the logic of the situation – then the irony of history will have come full circle.

That such sustained turmoil could persist despite the party leaders' usual insistence on absolute discipline is partly due to the party's own deepening internal differences. But the ultimate constraint on the Politburo is the ominous reality, as one astute Vietnamese once told me, that the army could never call upon its peasant soldiers to shoot other peasants. Any attempt to do so might very well fail, thereby endangering the party's very hegemony. Having initiated a fundamental change in the social relations touching the lives of three-quarters of the nation, the party has lost control over the peasants' responses to its inevitable and predictable traumatic consequences.

Rural inequality: the party and landlords

The immense problems in fixing rights and boundaries were certain to create interminable difficulties even under the best of circumstances. But the fact that one-fifth of the serious disputes resulted from the corruption of primary party cadres, and another 8 percent from conflicts between state organizations on land issues, has only greatly aggravated the party's incapacity to implement an already deeply flawed strategy.[10] It is clear from the party's own press that a significant fraction of the rural cadres, numbering a million persons, are taking advantage of the land transformation for their personal benefit, becoming a very large portion – perhaps the dominant one – of the landowners who are exploiting the peasants. In effect, as individuals' positions in the party become crucial to determining how the nation's land is divided, politics rather than efficiency is defining economic development. If anything delegitimizes the Communist party so that the masses openly oppose the state, this combination of factors is likely to be the cause.

Party leaders openly complain that a significant portion of the rural cadre

> do not do things democratically, and they act in an irresponsible manner . . . the work style of cadres in general is administrative and bureaucratic in nature. . . . [They] concentrate on engaging in economic activities for their families, [producing a] new authoritarianism.[11]

A considerable proportion are "taking much land for their own use, buying and selling property to make a profit."[12] Their housing is visibly much better and many are exploiting their administrative access to land and village funds. The party openly admits that "there are some hot spots that have arisen because some of the leading and managerial cadres at the primary level are corrupt and have violated the ownership rights of the people."[13] These abuses range from becoming large landowners themselves to imposing illegal taxes in districts they rule and illicitly selling land rights – and much more. The cadres, which is to say the state for practical purposes, are therefore the focus of many spontaneous protests.

This revision of the entire land system has been initiated at a structurally precarious time for agricultural labor. Vietnam's labor force is growing at about 3 percent a year, or more than one million persons. Low agricultural productivity means that the rural sector can absorb only about two-thirds of its share of this increase, producing a rising rural underemployment rate that was already 31 percent in 1993 – about five million persons. Although the urban areas cannot possibly absorb them, an increasing number are moving to cities, creating growing social problems.[14] These circumstances have combined with land changes to marginalize an important and growing sector of the peasantry, causing mounting inequality and a rural class structure in which landless-ness is an important feature.

Hired labor has therefore become a major factor in the rural social structure. Many peasants who own small amounts of land must supplement their income as hired laborers, and in some areas as many as two-thirds work for wages. Wherever the rural economy develops most quickly the demand for hired labor rises with it – precisely as the market ideology promised. The majority of the peasants do not produce a surplus of rice for the market, and of these a large minority do not even grow enough for subsistence. Forty to fifty percent of the households do not consume minimum basic diets. The wealthiest tenth of the peas-antry hire labor routinely, and those in the top quarter do so frequently. The party celebrates the fact that "the social structure of the countryside is changing, gradually giving rise to a class of middle peasants," and the logic of its stance is that a highly differentiated class structure is desirable because ostensibly it is, as the World Bank claims, more productive.[15] Given the surplus labor, and the fact there is no legislation whatsoever to protect them, hired workers can be exploited as badly as under the French, and in some places this is already occurring.[16] Meanwhile, al-though a substantial minority is prospering, a growing marginal-ized and displaced rural proletariat is also reemerging, and the party is oblivious to their dangerous political and social potential – one which the hot spots only reiterate. It has forgotten entirely that the oppressed may still recall the socialist rhetoric that is nominally the state ideology and turn it against their exploiters.

All surveys on rural inequality, despite their limits, agree that it is increasing quickly. The agrarian situation today is extremely fluid and all the factors that can produce even more inequality and make "greater land concentration and landlessness . . . likely to occur," as the World Bank optimistically predicts, have just come into play.[17] Well before 1993, detailed studies revealed that a sharp class differentiation was occurring in the land system, in part because of usury but also as a result of the new right of peasants to mortgage, and lose, what they possess; but wealthier peasants are also best able to produce for markets – especially if they are near cities. Rural society, which comprises four-fifths of the entire nation, is becoming significantly more like the one against which the Communists first mobilized the masses. Ngo Vinh Long has summarized this trend to show that some rural households earn forty times more than poor ones, with veterans and survivors of soldiers generally faring the worst and rural cadres being prominent among a new class that some land experts describe as "new local despotisms."[18]

Many wealthier landowners have diversified their operations to rent out farm equipment and offer essential services to poorer peasants, and, as under the French, they have decisive control over rural credit, both in terms of access to funds and the rates charged. Most peasants in every nation seek loans during the growing season, and credit is their most vulnerable point. Land systems historically become highly unequal, not because rich farmers produce better and more crops, as the World Bank argues, but principally because they capitalize on credit and its human consequences. In the end, Vietnam will have far more parasitism and social problems than – as the incredulous Politburo believes – food, and it will have all the problems of "market" agriculture and few of its alleged assets. When the party abandoned the existing land system it failed to create a substitute for the credit structures that the cooperatives had maintained. Moreover, the coops' essential social safety network to prevent peasants going into debt, above all because of illness, was also largely discarded, leaving even normally better-off peasants vulnerable to usury.

Government or regular banking sources, including coops that have since disappeared, claim to have provided 30 percent of the agrarian credit resources in 1993, though some estimates are only a third of that. The so-called informal sector, or usurers, who are generally large landowners, provide the larger part, and they usually charge at least three times the official interest. But the cheaper subsidized credit, as the World Bank reports, "does not end up benefiting the poor since influential households compete more successfully for these limited resources."[19] This often means the cadres. So the wealthiest eighth of the rural population in 1993 borrowed almost half of the low-interest loans and over half those from private sources. Very little credit is available to poorer peasants, and being high risks they pay far more. In some regions, over half the poorer farmers have already accumulated debts that amount to triple their assets, and their lives are entirely at the mercy of usurers. In effect, having freed agriculture and created all the factors that cause events to overwhelm peasants, the classic problems of a traditional rural society everywhere in the world are quickly reemerging. And since after 1993 household debt can legally be linked to land titles, defaults have already begun and far more are certain.

By 1993 it was obvious that the land reform was having an increasingly negative impact on about half of the peasants, who were either already worse off or were standing still while the security they had always enjoyed disappeared – leaving an ominous future. While the data leave much to be desired, an official analysis concluded that by mid-1993 only 22 percent of the farmers had improved their general financial position significantly; another, that a fifth of the farmers were relatively rich and a quarter were desperately poor – with all the variations in between. Sixty percent of the peasant families in 1992–3 were below the World Bank's absolute poverty standard.[20]

The new land system was organized to help the minority of better-off peasants prosper while the remainder were poised to lose; conditions for them could only deteriorate. To cope with this disturbing trend, the party in mid-1993 resolved to reestablish some of the cooperatives' functions. The coops had "played a great and important role in the struggle of national liberation," which was tantamount to declaring that now that the poor peasants were no longer needed to sacrifice for the cause they would be sacrificed to the laws of the market. While their "old functions . . . are no longer appropriate," new, more relevant roles for the coops had to be created.[21] But it admitted that the majority of coops had experienced great difficulties since 1988, and by 1993 five-sixths of them no longer existed in any form; crucial agricultural infrastructure responsibilities were being badly neglected: irrigation, production and marketing services, credit, technical education and improvements, and the like. It promised to remedy the situation. But no legal structure or guidelines for doing so existed and it revealed the intensity of its commitment by taking three more years to fill this crucial void, and even then much was left to be desired. At the June 1996 congress, the party admitted that the rural social system was in serious trouble and "measures must be taken against usury, pre-harvest purchases of paddy, and illegal land transactions."[22] It had severely gutted the coops within months; but assuming it was not already far too late, much less possible, it would require many years to restore their valuable functions. The belief that they could reconcile the market with equity revealed the utter naiveté of those calling themselves Marxists.

Opinion surveys among the peasants in 1993-4 confirmed that four-fifths wanted the coops to continue to take responsibility especially for vital irrigation services, which were being badly neglected, but also for marketing and buying. Indeed, to compensate for the huge void that the precipitous abandonment of the coop system had produced, peasants, especially in poorer areas, began to create voluntary associations to deal with common needs, such as water conservancy and crop protection. In 1994, 120 new coops and 10,000 producers' groups were formed. While this was still only a very small gesture, it revealed that many peasants desire protection from the market's fatal risks.

The fate of the coops points to several key challenges facing the leaders, not the least of which is that, while private land ownership exploited agriculture's immediate untapped productive reserve, this potential had inherent technical limits; when this short-term windfall ends the system's many social faults will increase faster than output. Even World Bank consultants by 1996 warned that "the country's agricultural sector was approaching capacity," and there was "little scope for further growth" unless major improvements were made in the entire infrastructure, rural credit, and extension services.[23] Only a third of the rice fields are irrigated, the rural road system has been largely abandoned, and, with the first flush of prosperity for a minority of peasants about over, the largest part of the consumer market will also begin to dry up.

The support that the peasants gave the Communist party after 1944 was the single most important reason for its success. They provided its strength and often compelled it to introduce reforms that broadened its popular appeal, in return for which they accepted and made monumental sacrifices. However elitist its top leadership, the party's triumph as a social movement was based largely on its responsiveness to the peasants' needs. For its present leaders to abandon this symbiotic relationship for one that can only drive an enduring wedge between the party and a large portion of the masses is to forsake the social rationale for its very existence. To function without the people under conditions that injure and increasingly alienate most of them may tempt the party to rely on repression to a far larger extent than it has ever done – but it too will fail eventually, and in the end the risks to the party vastly exceed all possible gains from the new land policy. It is impossible to tell how far its grave predicament has developed, or will go, but that it is already serious is unquestionable.

As a wounded war veteran put it, "In order to take the land from the hands of landlords, we lost half a century and paid with our sweat, blood, and bones. Now landlords are taking back the land. . . . "[24] The land issue is the greatest challenge confronting the Communist party, and if the trends of the past decade continue it will very likely lose its fatal gamble with the market. It is an issue that has deep social roots, and while the masses are today a long way from being out of control, a very significant portion is discontented and responding in unprecedented, direct ways. As injustice increases, as it must given the land system's structural flaws, the social basis for protest and the potential for a genuine mass movement will grow with it.

It would be both a consummate irony and a profound tragedy were the Communist party to initiate the class struggle all over again, but this time aligned with the oppressors rather than the oppressed.

Chapter 5

The social and human costs of reform

When Vietnam's leaders in 1986 initiated far-reaching political and economic policy changes, they scarcely considered the potentially enormous social and human consequences that abolishing the existing highly organized social security and welfare network could create. They were oblivious to the fact that a growing urban industrial working class might produce serious challenges if their basic needs were left unmet. Worse yet, they prepared to alter drastically the basis of the entire food system, insensitive to its possible impact in a food-deficit country if any of their crucial assumptions failed.

The Politburo could embark on the basic transformation of the social order with both profound naiveté and astonishing ignorance because its absolute authority insulated it from criticism or discomforting information. But the traditional distribution of social and economic benefits quickly changed profoundly and generated mounting problems that are irresistibly producing an inequitable class society. Originally, the party believed that prosperity would increase and benefit a growing share of the population. But as reforms moved from abstract theory to reality, a very different and seriously troubled society has emerged, increasingly threatening Vietnam's social cohesion. Meanwhile, the party's functional goal of economic development regardless of its human costs has conflicted with those egalitarian social ideals which have always been the very raison d'être for its existence.

THE QUALITY OF LIFE

The party officially urges that "all people in society and all party members should strive to amass wealth for themselves and for the nation as a whole," thereby "promoting economic growth," but it acknowledges that "it will be difficult to avoid gaps between rich and poor," which if not controlled "will lead to danger and social turmoil" – thereby threatening "social safety."[1] It has become hopelessly entangled in the contradictions between its ideological image of itself and its practice. Ironically, as if its original ideas will not be taken seriously by others and have no potential consequences, it continues to articulate those socialist values essential for mass resistance to the very society it is now constructing.

While economic inequality is difficult to measure anywhere, its general contours are reflected in the distribution of a nation's essential goods and benefits, of which food, housing, health, and education are the most crucial. Vietnamese experts' studies confirm that "social differentiation is rapid and that differences in income between household groups are quite extreme," and they are growing.[2] The income disparity between those labelled rich in 1993, or 4.1 percent of the families, and those 20 percent termed poor, was 13:1 in 1993, and twice as unequal if the divide between the very rich and very poor is measured. The gap since then has only increased.[3] The national distribution reflects the large difference between those who live in the urban as opposed to rural areas, as well as among the provinces, where growth rates are very uneven and inequality with the rest of the nation is growing. Ninety percent of the poor live in rural areas, and 60 percent of those in agriculture are poor compared to 19 percent of the white-collar workers and 14 percent of the government employees. By 1993, the most recent year available, the wealthiest tenth of the population received 29.0 percent of the income compared to 26.1 percent in France and 25.0 percent in the U.S. The wealthiest fifth received 44.0 percent, higher than many nations that have never pretended to be socialist. But since there is virtually no personal income tax, the after-tax share of the wealthy is far higher than in the industrial capitalist states. The poorest fifth received 7.8 percent of the income, less than in India and far less than even in Britain under Margaret Thatcher![4] Whatever its earlier problems,

Vietnam had always been a relatively highly equitable country. By 1993 the logic of the market had produced what was objectively a class society. This inequality has probably increased since then.

Rice: the great gamble

However useful Vietnam's own studies of social problems, they are less candid than the methodologically far-superior January 1995 World Bank report on poverty, which revealed that the government was underestimating seriously the magnitude of its failures. The Bank's report greatly embarrassed the regime, and proved that *doi moi* was failing insofar as public welfare was a criterion, and since then it has even ignored its own published data to assert that hunger has been reduced significantly. Indeed, in this as in other politically sensitive topics, Hanoi has doctored or misinterpreted data blatantly to prove that reforms are not creating mounting problems.

While the World Bank's estimates deal with the distribution of all basic necessities, it uses food as the principal criterion because it absorbs nearly three-fifths of all consumer expenditures. It classified 51 percent of the population in 1992–3 as "poor," and a quarter could not satisfy their daily essential calorie needs even if they spent all their money on food.[5] Counting consumption of every sort, nonfoods included, the wealthiest fifth of the population obtained over five times more per capita than the poorest fifth, with calorie intake almost twice as high. From this viewpoint, the government's figures on overall per capita rice production are misleading, since they obscure the deprivation inherent in existing inequality. But Vietnam's continuing, even worsening, food problem is to a very great extent the result of the government's dangerously irresponsible rice policy.[6]

Whatever their doctrinal differences, all socialists agree that their cause was intended to improve the people's livelihood, and there can be no better measure of welfare than food consumption. Reinforcing this commitment was the incontrovertible fact that food consumption must increase if a poor country is to develop. People who do not eat enough lack the energy that translates into human productivity, they learn much less quickly and have lower motivation, and their health suffers – generating a classic poverty syndrome that feeds upon itself. There is a huge economic cost, not to mention a social and moral one, to keeping food intake below an essential level, and whatever the short-term benefits from another strategy, in the end economic growth is seriously lessened and poverty protracted.

Of all the failures of the party's new strategy, none has been more harmful than its food strategy. As its leaders have abandoned their old principles, they have allowed food availability to decline to considerably below the supply that now exists. Whatever the problems before 1988, which reformers often exaggerated to justify their own program, it is the policy of claiming that there was a surplus of rice available for export, rather than the actual supply, that explains to a crucial extent why undernourishment and poverty have remained essentially unchanged since *doi moi* began.

As a peasant nation, the rice and food supply remains its primordial concern. Serious mistakes regarding it must affect the basic welfare of a majority of the nation. The difficulty in assessing Vietnam's rice situation is that neither outside analysts nor the nation's leaders have a sufficiently accurate grasp of the basic facts involving food stocks, a reality that is fraught with enormous risks. Just as the party during earlier decades released false data to vindicate its economic policies – a practice it later admitted – it has cited its alleged success in rice output and exports as confirmation of its wisdom. To admit failure in this domain would be to cast a very dark shadow on *doi moi*'s very raison d'être. At the beginning of 1996 the party daily newspaper revealed that official data on rice output "in recent years ... have been filled with inaccuracies, with the tendency being to exaggerate the achievements in grain production."[7] Previous reports of large successes in the crucial Mekong Delta were inconsistent with other information, including the failure of rice used for seed to increase significantly. Spot checks revealed that claims were 10 to 13 percent higher than actual yields. It was first discovered in 1994, and while no date is given for the inception of this monumental deception, it probably began much earlier. But such data had been used for six years to justify vast exports of rice needed urgently at home.

Since it began exporting rice in 1988, Vietnam has allowed its foreign exchange requirements to determine its exact export quotas. The surplus of any agricultural commodity cannot be estimated before the harvest, and reports on output were later exaggerated. From the viewpoint of real human needs, there has never been a sufficient amount, much less a surplus. Vietnam is far from being an adequately nourished nation. Rice prices have therefore consistently risen far more than other necessities, which has further reduced consumption.

Rice exports grew about 10 percent a year from 1989 to 1995, roughly twice the increase in paddy production, so that 7.4 percent of the entire reported crop was exported in 1989 and at least 12.4 percent in 1995. The state has greatly increased the incentive to the Chinese merchants, who largely control and profit the most from the trade, by permitting all foreign exchange earnings from rice to be used in full for imports, producing an automatic drain on the balance of payments. The rice commerce allows them to gain both ways, so that the nation's basic food source is being treated in an irresponsible, dangerous manner, the risks of which far exceed any potential benefits – save to the exporters. Beginning with 1.4 million tons in 1989, export targets were authorized at about 2 million tons in 1995. At the end of 1995, despite the fact that the annual yield had fallen 400,000 tons compared to 1994, an additional 150,000 tons for export were approved.[8]

As if this policy were not sufficiently risky, the state has no control over illegal exports, much of which, like the legal trade, goes to China, where rice fetches up to 30 percent more than in the domestic market but on occasion has even been double. Indeed, this price differential makes Vietnam extremely vulnerable to pressure were China to raise the price premium even further. While this large commerce is technically illegal, state agencies and even the military's own boats are deeply involved in it. The local parties in rice-surplus provinces simply ship directly to China. The volume of rice shipped illegally to China during the first half of 1995 was at least 700,000 tons, equivalent to the north's shortage due to a poorer harvest, and a considerable part of the rice sent north to relieve it ended in China. Although 2.15 million tons were authorized for export in 1995, the actual amount shipped was closer to 3 million – and 1996 was at least as high. To add to the difficulty of estimating rice consumption within Vietnam, up to one-quarter of the harvest is lost because of inadequate storage and harvesting. The UN's Food and Agriculture Organization at the beginning of 1995 stated that Vietnam, notwithstanding growing production, had not met basic food safety provision standards, and the government admitted as much by declaring later that year that it would set aside 100,000 tons, an utterly inadequate amount, "to cover any disaster or shortages."[9]

Rice was exported not only because the regime needed hard currency but also because consumer income has been too low to buy all of it. Meanwhile, as rice production was emphasized above all else, nonrice food output (including livestock) has been static since 1980. In light of all these facts and high population growth, a Vietnamese authority in early 1996 reported that "per capita rice consumption has declined, particularly in the cities." For nearly a decade the Politburo used inaccurate, possibly even deliberately falsified, data to justify its strategy, and the same source concluded that "the error is very large" in existing data and "could have a bad effect on our national grain safety, and there could be a repeat of the grain emergency."[10] These serious realities affecting the fundamental health and welfare of the masses can no longer be hidden.

While an exact calculation cannot be made, a reasonably plausible estimate of the magnitude of the party's food failure is possible. Using official data, rice output in 1995 fell 1.7 percent due to poor weather but exports increased about 20 percent, perhaps much more, and the population grew 2.2 percent. Ignoring wastage and exaggerated output figures, the remaining per capita rice supply was 272 kilos maximum. What is certain is that the average basic per capita food requirement is equivalent to 365 kilos, and were it met first there would be significantly higher economic productivity and superior health standards.[11] While the complexity and inconsistency of the criteria and data make it very difficult for outsiders to assess the truth, it is also impossible for the Politburo to avoid creating serious problems with its food policy. In addition to deceiving the public, many of its members are probably beguiling themselves as well, and no one should underestimate the sheer ignorance involved in the way it has defined major programs. Given Vietnam's declining control over the essential organizational and human factors, the potential for a grave food crisis is growing as the agricultural system continues to break down and the food-surplus areas, inspired by the party's appeal to enrich themselves, pursue their own interests.

Social services and human capital

While income inequality is translated initially into major differences in food consumption, it eventually affects housing, health, and education even more profoundly. Vietnam's basic human capital – once the highest of any East Asian nation – has been badly neglected even though it is an essential prerequisite for sustained, balanced economic development. When the party decided to apply strictly the IMF's macroeconomic guidelines in 1988, it slashed public sector spending so decisively that in 1996 even the IMF was mildly concerned about "a sharp deterioration in the quantity and quality of its education and health services. . . ."[12] While government statements on the social network exude optimism, the reality is that it is failing in terms of the quality of life of the masses. Everything that occurred after 1988 was predictable. What emerged is a pattern of winners and losers in what is rapidly becoming a class society like those everywhere.

There has been a serious decline in Vietnam's social services, beginning with health standards, since *doi moi* began. The DRV's health system was once as good as any in the region and better than most, but reunification confronted the north with a far inferior infrastructure in the south that was much too expensive to raise to its own standard immediately. *Doi moi* led to the introduction of expensive hospital and medical fees as well as to the collapse of the cooperatives that funded most local health care and education, and no public system replaced it. The south's medical structure failed to improve and the north's deteriorated quickly, and by 1994 the public health system provided under one-fifth of the medical services – even less than in Bangladesh, India, Indonesia, and Sri Lanka. In the region, only the Philippines spent less on public health as a proportion of the GNP, and India's outlay was over twice as high.

Public health, in effect, has been greatly reduced or abandoned altogether and Vietnam's public health services utilization dropped by over half between 1987 and 1994. The World Bank in 1993 characterized the unregulated private system as "poor." The remaining public structure was "dilapidated, poorly funded, and underutilized."[13] It was in crisis. Most government doctors earn $3–$12 a month, many have left the system, and the people have paid an immense price in personal suffering. The chances of a poor person in 1993 seeing a trained doctor when ill was less than

10 percent, but over 90 percent for upper income groups, and the per capita public health subsidy for those in the highest income fifth was even then six times that for those in the lowest. Public health, even after its drastic reduction, helps most those who can best afford private medicine. The public system since 1993 has declined even further, with minimum fees now payable by even the poorest. Naturally, there has been a sharp deterioration in health standards despite the fact that the number of medical personnel available in 1984 was very high by Asian standards. By 1996, the World Bank reported, "there is no system to assist the poorest."[14]

Given the official food policy, health must decline, and notwithstanding government exhortations, it is the state that is to blame, for "market" policies, as any Marxist should realize, have predictable social costs. The average weight and height of boys and girls has not increased and has probably fallen, and 45 percent of the children under five in 1989–95 suffered from malnutrition, about twice the rate for the entire Asian region. Nearly half the students in 1994 had spinal deformities. Health officials have publicly condemned food exports and the new health policy; had the nation been better fed, a very significant portion of the present medical emergency, with its innumerable short- and long-term costs, would have been avoided.[15]

The reappearance of prostitution is a shocking reflection of the failure of Vietnam's reforms. There were between 300,000 and 500,000 prostitutes in the south in 1973, and about 100,000 drug addicts. By 1993, there were over 200,000 unemployed young women in Ho Chi Minh City alone, and the police believed that about half of them worked as prostitutes, while health workers estimated that 600,000 women plied the trade nationally. In 1996 there were more prostitutes in Ho Chi Minh City than at the peak of the war. The official government data are far lower because it is an embarrassing reflection on its policies. Given prostitution's dependence on hotels and tourism, which cater to an increasingly explicit and lucrative sex trade, a significant number of police and party officials cooperate with it and take a share of the profits – almost none have been prosecuted for their role in what is highly visible commerce. In 1995 there were about 185,000 drug addicts nationally – almost twice the number in the south at the war's end. The result has been a debilitating health as well as social problem in the form of HIV, which will eventually reach the serious levels of the region's sex-tourism nations. There were 1,431 detected cases in May 1994, three times the number in June 1993; by the end of 1995 it had more than doubled again. Official edicts on confronting the disease have largely been ignored.[16]

Although Vietnam's health statistics are inadequate at best, the national trend is clear. As insecticide spraying and public health have declined, malaria, cholera, and dengue fever have grown. Access to safe water and sanitation was among the lowest in South and East Asia. Fewer than 1 percent of those in the poorest quintile have piped water in their home, compared with 37 percent in the highest. Waterborne diseases have been especially rampant among children, so many of whom are malnourished and have lower resistance than adults. At least 30 percent of children under five have acute respiratory diseases, and diarrhea is very common also. The general decline in health that all competent experts have repeatedly described is the logic of the party's increasing abandonment of its original social goals, and its tolerated official corruption and reduced services have intensified the problem. Faced with such a challenge, which involves the nation's morale as well as its health, the party has issued rhetoric that acknowledges the magnitude of the crises, as if it can play the diametrically opposed roles of sinner and saint simultaneously; but as one unofficial government official confessed in 1993, "social conditions have deteriorated in our country. If this problem exists for a long time, people won't believe in the Party and government any more."[17]

Vietnam's education system was once one of its greatest achievements, and from the viewpoint of economic development it created a potential for growth based on high skills that few poor nations possess. Its enormous superiority in human capital was crucial to its winning the war, but their infatuation with simplistic market theory after 1986 caused Vietnam's leaders to ignore the subtle but fundamental relationship between investment in the people's general welfare and economic growth. Cooperatives formerly paid 80 percent of the costs of the lower and middle schools, so schools were largely abandoned in many rural areas and buildings deteriorated; penurious wages forced many teachers to take other jobs. Most who remained are improperly trained, and have few options. And given the new land system, many parents now want (or require) their children to begin working earlier; the existence of many educated but under- or unemployed workers raises doubts about the justification of schooling.

Literacy rates are still high, but other nations in the region have about caught up with or exceeded them, and quality education has deteriorated quickly compared to the rest of Asia. After 1985–6, when a tuition system was instituted for nonprimary education, or education was privatized altogether, student enrollment declined sharply, especially in upper secondary and post-secondary schools, and the quality of what remains, including the primary schools, has been greatly reduced.[18] Advanced education fell even more dramatically, and the number of college students per 100,000 population in 1994 was about a tenth that of Thailand or the Philippines. The state still finances half of all expenditures on all education, but postsecondary education consumes much of it, and over two-thirds of the students who receive it come from the richest fifth of the families – and are principally children of party members. The aggregate per capita education subsidy for those in the wealthiest quintile is three times higher than for those in the poorest, thereby also institutionalizing the growing inequalities in the class structure.

"The impressive gains achieved during the last 30 years," the World Bank reported in 1993, "are under serious threat."[19] Many party members have openly "expressed grave concern about the current deterioration of our education system," but it continues to be sacrificed to the imperatives of a market system.[20]

WHICH SIDE ARE YOU ON? UNEMPLOYMENT AND URBAN LABOR

Unemployment data in most nations are tailored to serve political objectives, but Vietnam's also reflect the vast, complex human dislocations inherent in its transition from a socialist to a capitalist economy; they are, at best, very rough approximations. With *doi moi*, the government estimated that a quarter of the state sector's employees and one-fifth of the civil service were redundant, and the army was halved. Notwithstanding lofty rhetoric which the divisions within the party, its socialist pretensions, and public opinion demanded, the Politburo's decision to restructure the economy and the land system while slashing social security caused unemployment to rise sharply. From 1987 to 1992, total state employment fell by over one-quarter, or over 1.1 million people. The agrarian transformation began to increase landlessness – although still much less than will occur in the future. The growth of nonstate employment was large in percentage terms but it was insufficient to counterbalance other trends, including earlier school departures, and especially falling wages among those with jobs, which restricted consumer demand and the economic expansion dependent on it.

During 1989 and 1990, the most common estimate of unemployment was 20 percent of the labor force – mainly young people – but as many as one-third of those nominally working were on short hours. In late 1990, the army slowed demobilization because of a lack of jobs. Aware that the scale of unemployment would be used by antireform elements within the party, in early 1991 some official economists began to claim that unemployment was really only about a third of the 1989–90 estimates, but even they conceded that underemployment that year was at least 25 percent, and somewhat less thereafter. However, critical trade union economists believed the reality comprised "really worrying figures."[21] Urban unemployment in 1992 was at least 25 percent and has increased since, for population growth has far outdistanced new jobs. All such numbers do scant justice to real conditions, because most farmers, to take a key example, work fewer than 200 days a year, and many peasants, as in China, increasingly seek transient casual labor in the cities. More objective Asian Development Bank (ADB) estimates are that only half the annual 1.2 million young entrants into the labor force are finding jobs, and the ADB calculated general unemployment at 20 percent in 1993.[22]

When the party applied the IMF's draconian structural adjustment formula it was essential that real labor costs be lowered so that Vietnam's major "comparative advantage," as the Fund promised, would attract large foreign investments and make its processed exports attractive – neither of which has occurred. Far more important, however, was cheap labor's importance to domestic industrial development. Significant capital investments were not available, and if both the private and state industries and services were to prosper, reducing the cost of labor was the only certain way for them to do so. The remarkable success of both of these sectors since 1988, especially when compared to China and Russia, is due overwhelmingly to the intensified exploitation of the workers, and the leaders of the "party of the proletariat" made it a crucial aspect of the market strategy. "Vietnam," the IMF concluded in mid-1996 about its performance until then, "had the most success in reducing its real wage bill ... increases in nominal wages [were] below inflation. . . ."[23] The workers were squeezed – very hard.

Given the persistent downward trend in real income since 1985, employment per se has meant much less in social terms. Measurements of real income are elusive anywhere, but the general pattern is unmistakable. A wage freeze was imposed in the government sector after 1989, and given inflation and the elimination of subsidies, the real wages of state workers from 1985 through 1992 fell by about 50 percent. After 1992, the real wages of workers in both the foreign-owned and state industries fell about another one-third by the end of 1995. For all employed workers as a general group, the government has released data showing that from September 1993 to early 1996 real income fell by at least around 30 percent.[24] If measured over a decade, this decline has been extremely severe and long-lasting; even IMF experts have publicly expressed their anxiety concerning such strong measures "testing the will of authorities to 'stay the course' and eroding popular support for the reform process."[25] In fact, as I discuss below (pp. 114–18), ultraexploitation is already doing just that.

Real wages are much more significant than the nominal minimum wages which have been fixed at a monthly level and proven largely meaningless both because of inflation and because there is no effective limit on the hours labor is compelled to work. The government has admitted that under the present arrangement "the minimum wage in effect benefits the employers."[26] Hoping to attract foreign investment with the lowest wages in Southeast Asia, the Politburo in May 1992 reduced what was in fact an unenforced minimum wage in only foreign-owned plants from $50 a month for unskilled workers to $35 in Hanoi and Ho Chi Minh City and $30 in rural areas, even though the new rural standard was generally still far higher than the actual wages paid. But the minimum wage in state enterprises at the end of 1993 was equal to $11, significantly lower than the average $16 actually paid, and for practical purposes there is no minimum wage in the locally owned private sector. But while the dollar equivalent of wages has risen since 1993, inflation has more than neutralized it and real wages have continued to decline. Actual working conditions are often shocking, with forced and often unpaid extensions of the working day, delays in paying wages, the absence of benefits, and the physical and verbal abuse of workers – especially in foreign-owned plants. In May 1996 a government institute reported that over half of industrial labor – most of whom were in state firms – worked in hazardous conditions and the situation was only becoming worse with time. The party celebrates this degradation of a very large section of the nation's workers as "modernization and industrialization."[27]

These appalling circumstances are not only poor by world criteria: above all, they are intended to be.[28] Given the draconian situation in the work place itself, the fate of labor under those who rule purportedly in its name must go down as one of the most bitter ironies in the history of Communist parties. The majority of the Politburo, blindly infatuated with market theory which even embarrassed many nineteenth-century English conservatives as immoral, accepts and protects draconian wages in the naive hope that it will lead to rapid development. Do Muoi has consistently stated that

the worker class must support and encourage the business owners to become more confident in investing and expanding their production and business ... to create more jobs, [and] enrich themselves and the fatherland. . . .[29]

The proletariat, he noted in March 1996, had "manifested its fine nature by placing its interest after the common interests of the nation and people."[30] This ruthless, cynical evocation of the litany of socialist rhetoric to rationalize the optimum exploitation of the working class, perhaps as much as any issue, has split the party in two: a large majority composed of utterly cynical technocrats (as in the case of Prime Minister Vo Van Kiet) and dogmatic ideologues who believe this stage of forced accumulation must inexorably end well, and a small but articulate minority who retain traditional socialist values and realize that there is a limit to how far workers can be oppressed before they resist and produce social instability. For the minority, who are probably growing stronger, this can only aggravate further the party's delegitimation.

The party has put itself in an insoluble trap in its relation to industrial workers. It wishes foreign investors to take advantage of Vietnam's principal competitive advantage, and it has largely unsuccessfully attempted to entice them at the expense of workers who are publicly referred to as "a commodity."[31] Meanwhile, state-enterprise managers are being called upon to show a profit at virtually any cost, and to attain ever-higher growth – for which, as every Marxist knows, workers must pay. When the "market system under state management" began, party leaders anticipated social unrest where workers were laid off or, as was becoming widespread for periods of four months or even longer after 1988, not paid at all.[32] The IMF was asked to provide emergency loans to pay workers who refused to work for nothing. With high unemployment, however, labor remained reasonably docile.

There is hardly any area of the overall reform program that has succeeded in the way promised by those who advocated it. The growing waste and debilitation of human capital, juxtaposed against mounting social inequities, corrupt cadres, and high-living nouveaux riches, has produced the fundamental dilemma of how alleged socialists should react when the oppressed, mal-treated masses begin to respond – as they inevitably must any-where. While labor protest is only now beginning, it will un-questionably increase in the future, and even the most paranoid leaders will not be able to attribute it to mysterious "hostile forces."[33] The party ultimately cannot escape the responsibility for its own actions.

Strikes and unions: muzzling labor

Given the deepening dissent within its ranks over the place of superexploitation and rising discontent among workers, the party has been compelled to finesse its stance since 1992, but in essence it still strives to keep labor cheap. Its ostensible ideology requires it to maintain the façade of an official trade union, but the party strictly controls its functions and the labor market. Independently of attracting foreign investors, which is an economic matter, for political reasons it cannot permit autonomous trade unions to

protect the workers' interests. To accept them would be tantamount to breaking the party's monopoly of power.

To find a way between its elitist preferences, a critical minority
in the party, and growing worker dissatisfaction, eventually the
Politburo produced a sham labor code. In December 1992 the
government promulgated a ruling that collective agreements in
private Vietnamese and foreign factories (excluding state-owned
factories, those which involved the military, and the civil service)
could be formed if an officially approved union representing more
than half the workers were created or, much more ambiguously,
a body claiming to represent workers were formed where no
union existed. The latter, in effect, could preempt independent
worker organizations if necessary, but in either case the local
government office would determine if an agreement was valid –
giving it final control. No guaranteed workers' prerogatives or
protection, including the freedom to strike, existed beyond these.
In theory, their rights to organize were to be respected, but in
reality at the government's discretion.

But the matter could not rest there because, despite high
unemployment, in February 1993 the largest strike in Ho Chi Minh
City's history broke out – a wildcat strike of over 600 workers
against a Korean–Vietnamese joint venture. The issues were low
pay, excessive hours, and managers who beat workers: all those
conditions necessary to make profits rise quickly and attract
foreign capital. In this case, after two days the company merely
agreed to pay the minimum wage and to accept a union under the
vague new rules. In fact, 14 percent of the private firms in the city
already had official unions which, given the restraints on them
and the labor market, were purely ceremonial. But even so, at least
twenty strikes occurred in Ho Chi Minh City during 1992–3. The
state's dilemma was plain: if workers were treated more decently,
foreign investors would be deterred. But if it failed to do anything,
autonomous workers' unions might fill the vacuum. Which side
would the "party of the proletariat" be on?[34]

The party attempted to straddle the fence for as long as possible.
Once strikes were allowed, some leaders asked, where would they
end, with the clear implication that strikers might be social
enemies in disguise. Besides, to reach socialism according to the
new doctrine's road map, it was necessary first to pass through
capitalism – capitalists by definition must exploit, and strikes
would discourage them. At the January 1994 party conference, Do

Muoi phrased the characteristically evasive dialectical line, in which opposites were united: there would be laws "to protect the legitimate interests of both employees and employers," taking into account "investment promotion, the elimination of social injustice, and opposition to illegal businesses."[35]

The labor law approved by the National Assembly in June 1994 was hotly debated publicly and generated profound differences. If elements of the working class begin to chafe against official constraints, repression would only encourage independent labor organizations to emerge, and they in turn would seriously erode the party's ideological legitimacy. The potential dangers of this trap are all too obvious, but were the official union to begin to side with the workers they might be circumvented. Sensing this, a significant portion of the traditionally docile government trade union openly criticized the state's wage and social security policies, cautiously aligning itself with the opposition.

Meanwhile, the new law bans all strikes in public services and, much more vaguely, in "major enterprises essential to the national economy or national security."[36] Apart from its time-consuming conciliation procedures, it outlaws independent unions and unauthorized strikes; in those undefined industries where workers are ostensibly free to strike and vote to do so, only the executive committees of local unions can decide if they may actually strike – and that is not intended to occur. Leaders of illegal strikes are explicitly subject to dismissal and prosecution! The law contains no rules on overtime pay, night- and piecework, forms of payment, or much else that is important to workers. Social insurance rights for practical purposes are unenforceable. The assumption is not that unions and companies will negotiate but that companies will merely apply state-imposed criteria and decisions. The Politburo conceded a nominal freedom it expected would rarely, if ever, be exercised. Meanwhile, the party's own divisions on this crucial issue have widened, causing it to lose the total control over the working class it has always had – and requires.

Essentially, the labor code has remained a façade, mainly because it was not intended to reform the situation but also because the official union, despite significant internal differences, is unprepared ultimately to resist the Politburo directly. If it does not attempt to find a solution that gets workers back on the job, the very best the union can do is remain passive and allow the workers to fight for themselves against the bosses alone, without fear of the official unions. This in fact frequently occurs. But the official unions themselves have done little to protect workers before strikes occur. By early 1996, only 12 percent of the private sector work force was in unions, but not one wholly foreign-owned enterprise had a union – this would only deter investors. Party critics of the Politburo's line have published exposés of the labor code as a dead letter and of the official union executives as having "failed to play their role well."[37] Since the worst abuses – from beatings, forced overtime, and unsafe conditions to with-holding pay – have occurred in joint ventures and foreign-owned plants (especially Korean) that expect to make the most of Viet-nam's promised comparative advantages, they have experienced the most labor disputes. Many cadres assigned to protect their workers, as the government has publicly admitted, "have turned their backs on their own compatriots . . . because they have been given high pay by their foreign bosses."[38]

Strikes have varied greatly in size and duration. An initial official estimate of at least 214 strikes nationally from 1989 to March 1996 is too conservative. The union paper reported thirty-two strikes in the first ten months of 1994 alone. There were "dozens" of unauthorized strikes in 1995, the party admits publicly, nearly double the number in 1994 – and even more in 1996.[39] These strikes technically are all independent of the official union. Given the party's refusal to inhibit foreign investors, and its desire to encourage the rich to grow richer, strikes will continue to grow in the future. Critics within the official union predicted that "labor disputes and contradictions between workers and management will increase and, in some localities and sometimes, will get more bitter."[40] Notwithstanding its fear that "foreign investment will not come to Vietnam," the labor ministry in April 1996 finally attempted to preempt this mounting pressure by raising the minimum wage in foreign companies alone by $10 a month, although some refused to pay it; but it ignored the many other grievances that workers have regarding conditions, and it did nothing for the great majority who are not in foreign-owned plants.[41]

Despite the Politburo's intentions and the fact that all the strikes before and since 1994 were illegal from a procedural viewpoint, they have become more frequent and evoke increasing sympathy in the official press. Above all, no prosecutions have been reported. The implications of such open resistance to the official line should be neither overstated nor minimized, but there is no precedent for it. For a party that aspires to impose total control, it is a very uncomfortable exception. Elements within the masses and the party itself have acted on behalf of an independent position on social equity, and the Politburo has so far not dared to use its power against them. It tolerates antisocial corruption, and it will endanger its authority profoundly if it imposes its will only over eminently justified mass grievances. But the very conditions the party has created in its effort to industrialize the nation by ruthlessly driving the workers virtually assures that there will be more confrontations between labor and capital, with the party aligned with the latter. It is caught in a trap between its ideology and its desires.

After a decade of ad hoc improvisations, the party's leaders can no longer avoid the glaring contradictions between their founding doctrine and the exploitative imperatives of "market socialism," nor the mounting social consequences of their new order. As in the countryside, the people are being compelled to act without the party's authority, if not against it. Both its own corrupt cadres and, increasingly, the masses are defying the basic Leninist organizational demand for discipline, intensifying the party's delegitimation in the eyes of urban workers. This incremental process is not producing a single major challenge to which the regime can reply, but a long sequence of relatively minor events whose cumulative significance could very well become formidable.

If in the future the Politburo attempts to reestablish its hegemony, it may find its power overtaken by events and sorely tested. But if it does not, it will be – as in many other domains – increasingly bypassed. It is not an enviable dilemma for it to be in.

Chapter 6

Who rules, and why?

The Communist party on the threshold

The Vietnamese Communist party was founded with the mission to construct a social order based on justice and equality, and it created an idealistic vision that persuaded countless men and women to dedicate their lives to a cause that transcended their immediate personal interests. What the party now denigrates as "voluntarism" was the single most important source of its members' intense devotion and incredible sacrifice, without which it would have lost the war. This ideological legacy remains the party's official doctrine, and many of its members, especially the older ones, still tenaciously, passionately believe in it. Without it, indeed, they cannot justify their enormous privations – and their entire lives' very purpose. To a great extent, the Communist party as an institution remains deeply constrained ideologically, and the growing disparity between its values and reality has created a profound crisis of identity. Although many of the party's key leaders by the mid-1990s had forgotten its socialist objectives, it cannot easily abandon the faith which united it for half a century and led to its greatest triumph.

After a decade of market reform, Vietnamese society has begun to assume a fairly cohesive institutional form that resembles socialism less and less, and this has resulted in a critical debate within an increasingly divided Communist party unable to bury its ambitious ideological heritage. Its dictatorship failed to create an equitable, just society, either in deed or in inspiration.

To comprehend Vietnam at the present moment requires us to compare the Communist party's image of itself, with its plethora of rhetoric, aspirations, and theory, against reality. Differentiating between ideology and actuality is mandatory everywhere, of course, but the gap between existence and assertions about it are much greater in Vietnam than in most cases because it is ineluctably marching toward a society radically different than that the party set out to create fifty years ago. To the extent its members recognize that socialism is being betrayed, there is a growing danger that conflict within the party itself could destroy the consensus-based system that has always united it.

The official Communist position is that Vietnam is still committed to creating a socialist society, although its definition of the goal has become increasingly vague and divorced from socialism interpreted in terms of explicit institutions and social relations. Indeed, socialism is now even being depicted as the objective of charity. As the youngest and most promising Politburo member characterized it in mid-1996, "In Vietnam, we say 'let those who have favorable conditions enrich themselves first, and then let those less fortunate enrich themselves later, thanks to the support of those who have already become rich'."[1] On the other hand, the International Monetary Fund, after more than a decade of direct control over its economy, in 1996 described Vietnam as a model for implementing its criteria – which have always been hostile to socialism:

Vietnam today stands on the threshold of a new era. . . . After almost a decade of concerted efforts, its economy and finances have been substantially reformed, and it is firmly integrated into the world economy. . . . The momentum of change – guided by market principles and buoyed by strong growth – seems irreversible.[2]

We cannot believe both the IMF and those who insist that Vietnam is still a socialist society, and it is essential to juxtapose reality, in terms of the control and distribution of economic resources, against rhetoric and myth. At some point, false images of the world no longer suffice, save insofar as they tell us something about those who either believe or propagate them. Resolving this question is also now the most crucial issue facing the Communist party, which since 1994 has increasingly been undergoing a bitter debate concerning the nation's direction.

WHO RULES? WHO GAINS? THE PARTY AND THE CLASS STRUCTURE

An accurate assessment of Vietnam's evolving class structure must first identify those who have obtained most from a decade of "market socialism" and their precise social and political origins and relationship to those whom the party now holds "in high esteem."[3] No less crucial is the extent to which those at the top of the economic hierarchy are there because they have made a positive contribution to economic growth, and the degree to which they really are a parasitic manifestation of the corrupt sector of the Communist bureaucracy – creating what is often described, for lack of a better term, as "bureaucratic capitalism." In a word, is the Communist party in its late and perhaps last stage employing its power and prestige to annex the hybrid it now euphemizes as a "market-oriented structure ... under socialist direction," exploiting it for the personal advantage of its own members?

In terms of the actual benefits from government spending on all social transfers and education, health, and the like, party members have received by far the most. Vietnam's social security system covers only state-sector (principally government) employees in a comprehensive manner, and only a tenth of the labor force is eligible for much-reduced benefits. Government workers, who are overwhelmingly party members, receive over four-fifths of all social security payments and have a far lower rate of poverty – 14 percent in 1993 – than any occupational category. They comprise a large portion of the wealthiest fifth of the population, which receives 38 percent of all social transfers and 44 percent of the income. The per capita education subsidy for those in this top group is three times higher than for the poorest, and the public health subsidy is six times more.

The party after 1954 created a system that was both organized and informal for retaining social and political power in the hands of its original members, their families, and their descendants. The majority of the advanced educational opportunities were reserved for their children, and the second and third generations who eventually took over were qualified far less by their technical, bureaucratic competence, in the formally neutral Weberian sense, than by their social and family ties, which became a prerequisite for entering the bureaucracy. They were trained, of course, but this system gave mediocrity and nepotism a decisive preference over talent. When joining the party, children and siblings of existing members were admitted without investigation, and naturally they swelled its ranks. Separate schooling encouraged intermarriage, and the party in most locations, especially urban, is a distinct social, educational, and political caste. It was inevitable that such intimate family and personal ties would produce the new economic elite that was encouraged after 1986.[4] Their head start was decisive.

The wealthiest classes since 1986 are concentrated principally in cities: especially the Saigon area, where local Chinese are dominant, and in Hanoi, where there is far less opportunity for normal economic development but where access to political and bureaucratic power – involving state favors, illegal land transfers, and corruption in general – compensates for the north's poverty. One Vietnamese study of families in Hanoi classified as "rich" in 1992 found that almost all the heads of these families had university degrees, which meant they were overwhelmingly privileged party families. Over half of them had one or more parent working for the state, four-fifths of whom were senior cadres at a very high level, principally in agencies where both domestic and foreign economic affairs were handled. "Conditions such as these permitted these families to become rich," the report concluded.[5]

Even before these results were released in mid-1995, the party was admitting that "most of these private businessmen are intellectuals and educated people, among them cadres, party members, and revolutionary families."[6] Nepotism, probably even more than in China, has been the single most important (but certainly not the only) mechanism since the mid-1980s in defining the way the "market" is replacing the "socialist" economy. To this extent, most of the new entrepreneurs are really inheriting and exploiting the transitional economy rather than creating new wealth in the nominally "objective" apolitical manner hypothesized in laissez-faire theory. Because their strong personal ties to the existing political elite make it unlikely that they will attempt to transform their economic power into political power before the older generation steps down, the political and economic elites trust each other. While the system is changing, the rulers are largely identical, and continuity is the leitmotif.

This favoritism is very blatant and inevitably became a source of great tension within the party, and about 1994 the Politburo commissioned a study of how to reconcile it with socialist principles. In the spring of 1996, before the party congress, the delicate problem was still unresolved, and those hostile to the market line focused repeatedly on party members, but especially their wives and children, who have become capitalists. If they were forbidden to do so, there would be a profound alteration in the nation's economic elite, and there was simply no way this could occur without a very serious split in the party. Indeed, in certain ways this is potentially one of the most divisive issues confronting the party, for it involves both money and families, subjects that cause passions to run high. This sensitive issue exposed the reformers as avaricious and self-interested, and their critics forced them on the defensive. But in the end, typically, the Politburo obfuscated the situation. Ignoring the crucial question of families entirely, it simply declared that party members should "refrain from exploitation and private capitalist economy," just as they should cease being corrupt.[7] Families were implicitly exonerated from all restraints, but it quickly emerged that even the ban on party members would not be very strict, much less enforced. In principle, household businesses were permissible, and when asked about it, Do Muoi shrugged and observed that "some [members] will do their business. It's a matter of your stomach."[8]

The Politburo's dilemma is that a very significant number of the party's members are corrupt – only a tenth of them, and it is certainly higher than that, would amount to 220,000 – but also their families are often decisively linked to their peculations, and purging them would destabilize the increasingly delicate political balance within the entire party. Coalitions based on reciprocal favors could easily capsize on this point alone. Many loyal, sincere Communists who made immense personal sacrifices for the struggle have tolerated, if not aided, their children's corruption but do not regard such favoritism as truly unethical; indeed, some consider denying their children advantages as even more immoral. As everywhere where corruption becomes an integral aspect of economic activity, concepts of legality are freely adapted to imperative human, personal relations. Past and present Politburo members themselves, especially Prime Minister Vo Van Kiet, have been accused publicly of protecting their families and friends engaged in massive corruption. The assets of Vietnam's allegedly richest businessman in 1996, Le Van Kiem, were based principally on land he obtained from the state for a fraction of its value and contracts he has obtained from it since. He is also a crony of Kiet and his key deputy, Phan Van Khai, an arch-technocrat and Politburo member who is the other eminence grise of the market strategy. Indeed, Kiem has been publicly identified as serving principally as a front for government officials.[9]

Roughly one-quarter of the nation has unquestionably prospered since 1988 in a sustained, significant manner, and they have gained by far the most from reform. This stratum comprises the Chinese commercial elite in the south but principally the much more numerous party members who have exploited their political leverage, usually at the local level. Most are small operators; indeed, many are not so much greedy as obliged to supplement their paltry official income, and they are not insatiably corrupt or ambitious. Children of party families, who joined not out of belief but necessity, are more acquisitive, but the family and personal ties of the new entrepreneurial and wealthy class are its single most defining characteristic. Without them, the majority of those who have been successful would have fared far more poorly. Five percent of the entire nation over twenty-four years old belong to the party, but about one-sixth of all urban adults are party members, so that most of the new rich who live in towns, above all in the north, are linked to it directly or indirectly.

In effect, the party's own members largely lead the "market," and entrepreneurship in the economy is an integral extension of their political power. Just as Vietnam's variety of "socialism" bears scant relationship to Marx's original concepts and Ho Chi Minh's definitions of them, its "market" economy scarcely resembles Adam Smith's theory or that now being celebrated with the IMF's rhetoric. What is clear is that those who reigned as Marxist-Leninists still rule, and profit, from the economic mutation that has emerged from that ideological tradition. Doctrine is far less the motive of action than greed. In a world whose inordinately complex historical experiences have bypassed all of the nineteenth century's conventional theories and wisdom, it is less useful to try to label this mutation in traditional terms than to understand it for its power relationships. What is central is the continuity of personnel and authority within a labyrinthine configuration of nominal ideas that are banal and cynically devised, and are abandoned when they are no longer utilitarian. They cannot be dignified as concepts intended to have inherent significance or coherence, or reflecting deeply held beliefs. That would only give them an undeserved benefit of the doubt.

THE POLITBURO AND DISSENT

Much of the confusion in the party's position – its optimism and pessimism, and its conflicting impulses to encourage both creativity and discipline in one and the same policy document – has been due to the Politburo's increasing penchant for combining irreconcilable ideas in the futile hope that it can resolve its growing disagreements. Its most important statements are usually obviously inconsistent and offer no coherent guidelines, so that local and provincial parties can interpret them as they wish – encouraging Vietnam's inherently fissiparous tendencies. But whatever its own nominal differences, which have grown since 1985, virtually all Politburo members agree that they must, above all, safeguard their own domination, with far less deference to the desires of the lower ranks or masses than they dare to admit. Nguyen Van Linh, the secretary-general until June 1991 and ostensibly the leading reformer, initially attempted in minor symbolic ways to reverse the party's corruption, stale rhetoric, and general bureaucratic malaise, and most members welcomed his refreshing candor. But he was astonishingly naive about economics, and initiated "market" reforms expecting that the IMF's ideology would prove valid in ways Leninism had never been. Although honest and sympathetic, he soon became a political compromiser, loyal to the existing power structure, ultimately reflecting the party's profound confusion rather than overcoming it.

The doctrine of its absolute supremacy and infallibility that the Politburo has enshrined is becoming an illusion; the provincial parties increasingly ignore it, and it cannot impose control on many party members. While claiming to be unified, the party is functionally "pluralist" in the sense that significant power groups operate independently of each other, not with differing ideological goals but rather for wealth and power translated into both material gains and autonomy for their regions. The Politburo's most serious challenge today comes not from outside the party but from the lower organizations within it.

Democracy and human rights are inextricably linked to the party's inability to define viable socialist economic policies, for they are the precondition for its long-term survival. The party's factions have responded to these topics in a manner that has muddled the relationship between such crucial issues almost beyond comprehension. But in principle the party has for decades accepted the necessity of internal criticism and democracy, and in the several years after it embarked on *doi moi* it appeared to be willing to accept it in fact as well; as late as March 1989, its formal position was to "encourage freedom of speech [and] promote straightforward discussion and debate," although even then it warned against these rights leading to what it called "sabotage."[10] From the inception, the compromises that the senior leaders struck on these issues were full of obvious and irreconcilable tensions between freedom and control. What emerged was a plethora of contradictions and banal rhetoric. Democracy, they stated, was to be implemented through much greater economic freedom, and by the party, state, and political system operating in a self-renewing manner, a goal which they have consistently admitted has not been attained.

Since the party openly acknowledges that corruption and bureaucracy have only increased and now pose the greatest and most imminent threat to its future, its fundamental and immediate task is to restore its own health very quickly. But other than making futile exhortations, it has been unable and unwilling to do so. At the same time, it refuses to accept the principle that critics within the party itself may not only speak, for they are already highly vocal, but also operate as organized groups to attain their goals. Ironically, by making its own hegemony more important than resolving the party's crisis, the Politburo is most likely to erode the party's legitimacy and original socialist goals – and, ultimately, its own power. Its use of authority to defend abuse and exploitation can only lead to utter cynicism and growing hostility toward the Communist party.

The extent to which the Politburo would unite against rare dissenters in its own midst was reflected in the affair of Tran Xuan Bach, who ranked as member number nine, was head of the foreign affairs department, and was far better informed on Soviet-bloc and international questions than anyone. Many serious critics within the party, who were more optimistic in the late 1980s, pinned their hopes on him, and Bach favored a far more extensive reform of the political structure than anyone with his power dared to accept. In January 1990 he declared "support for the democratization process in East Europe"; three months later he was expelled from the Politburo, and the crackdown on party dissidents accelerated.[11] His peers by that time had become increasingly frightened of changes in the former Communist world and restricted the notion of reform essentially to those economic innovations that are leading Vietnam to capitalism.

Far better known was the case of Bui Tin, deputy editor of the party daily, whom the BBC interviewed in France at the end of 1990 and who claimed: "I long for a humanist, modern, and pluralist socialism," "genuine socialism" rather than the version that existed.[12] In March 1991 he was expelled from the party and he remained in exile. In the subsequent tawdry exchanges between Hanoi and Tin, both sides distorted the truth grossly, which flattered neither of them. The party refused to admit that Tin had once been an exceptionally important senior cadre who had assumed major responsibilities during the war and was a favorite of Ho Chi Minh. To confess that it had placed enormous confidence in an apostate would have reflected poorly on its own judgment. Tin, for his part, had a monumental ego and was irate because he had not been given far more power, and after 1991 he openly condoned much of what the U.S. had attempted in Vietnam during the war, revealing his great personal instability. The affair reflected very badly on everybody.[13]

A brief but significant challenge to the regime was the creation of the Club of Former Resistance Fighters in Ho Chi Minh City in 1987. Their best-known leader, General Tran Van Tra, had in 1975 been commander of a vast region in the south and had already shown his independence through the unauthorized publication of his remarkably critical memoir on the end of the war. The club mobilized over 100 retired senior generals, officials, and others, and immediately supported a democratized party, allying itself with Tran Xuan Bach. It began a magazine in September 1988, which was soon confiscated. The club quickly spread throughout the south among disgruntled veterans and might have become a major focus of opposition, for while it began as a regional body its appeals were potentially much wider and no one could challenge easily its prerogative to question the way the system operates. And since economic reforms have hurt them badly, undermining the interests of those who sacrificed the most to achieve victory, the Politburo foresaw serious dangers ahead. In the spring of 1990 an alternative, sanctioned veterans' organization was created which serves as a mouthpiece for official policy. Tran Van Tra accepted the change reluctantly, but Nguyen Ho, a key club member who wrote a powerful indictment of the state, was placed under house arrest in September 1990 for attempting to keep the original organization alive. Since then, several dozen key dissidents within the party have been harassed and confined, and in November 1995 at least two senior party members who advocated a genuinely free debate were sentenced to prison for about a year. Although these groups have not become an organized opposition within the party itself, they reflect a larger tendency – Communists whose revolutionary credentials cannot be questioned. While they have only occasionally protested publicly against corruption since 1990, this potentially major constituency exists in the background, critical of those who are making a mockery of their enormous sacrifices.

Writers and intellectuals have been much more vocal in opposing party leaders. After *doi moi* there was something of a rapprochement between the two forces, and intellectuals were treated much more solicitously than the press – which has far more influence on the people. Underground tracts attacking the party appeared, and their access to official journals also made intellectuals a continual nuisance. Nguyen Khac Vien, the best known of them, in February 1991 called for a democratic society and the resignation of the party's leaders; and in June 1992, Tran Van Giau, Vietnam's leading historian and a personality of enormous prestige and influence, publicly excoriated the party chiefs as exponents of tired platitudes. Since then the official party has wavered between the carrot and the knout, but the publication of Bao Ninh's remarkable novel in 1991 – an unrelenting, powerful rejection of official party myths about the war and a reflection of the deeply alienated veterans' attitudes toward postwar realities – indicated that it had been compelled to leave the door slightly open to genuine opposition, above all from veterans. In this case, the book was a best seller and was awarded the Writers Association national prize, and there have been others just as unsparing.

After the party promulgated *doi moi*, a spate of unlicensed newspapers – perhaps half the total existing – were created, and in 1987 about two-fifths of all books published were unauthorized. Conforming to the reform's initial promises, newspapers were deluged with complaints, and many lower-level officials were castigated and some expelled – although senior party members were spared. By late 1989 the government decided to put "an end to the chaos" and "ideological confusion," cracking down strongly on the press and imposing increasingly rigid controls on it – although these were eventually relaxed substantially.[14]

Far more serious is the popular cultural challenge to the party's image of the quality of life it would like to see either preserved or created. What happens among the intelligentsia is far more easily regulated than the people's daily existence, and it is in this domain that the party has lost control entirely. Given the impact of its policies in devaluing Communism's appeal and causing wide-spread joblessness, especially among younger people, Buddhism has experienced a major resurgence for much the same reasons as Islam has among the masses in the Muslim world. Buddhists have created large organizations and the government has restrained some forcibly – there have been arrests and even some clashes – but it tolerates purely religious work, which has flourished in the moral and ideological vacuum the party has produced. Religion has the potential to reach the masses in a way that more elegant, formal ideas cannot. It could eventually confront the party with a very serious opposition, but this will depend largely on the success of its reforms and especially employment opportunities for young people.

A much greater danger than religion is the way that a significant portion of those under thirty-five years have become hedonists with a vengeance: conspicuous consumers of Coca-Cola and Honda racing motorcycles, who have no values to inhibit them from a riotous lifestyle that has imposed cacophony on life in the cities. At the beginning of 1996 the Politburo ordered a much-publicized campaign against "social evils and cultural poisons," mainly in the form of billboards and advertising, but few took it seriously. These threats were far more a reflection of the party's inability to provide a sense of purpose to people's lives than, as it fancies, alleged foreign plots. But even at the peak of its puritanical campaign during the months leading up to the June congress, it allowed both Texas Burgers and Kentucky Fried Chicken to open outlets, and even a bowling alley was established! The party's reformers also cynically pay lip service to ascetic virtues, but they really regard consumerism as an incentive to aggressive accumu-lation, and this explains why it flourishes unabated. The party remains trapped by the contradiction between its ideology and its commitment to the market, and it refuses to acknowledge the irreconcilable tension between them.

The party divided

Whatever the long-term risks of aggressive cultural pollution among younger people or the growth of religions, it is the increasingly profound division within the party's own ranks that has created the most immediate and dangerous threat to its transition toward an openly class society. Since about 1993, much more significant opposition to the Politburo's market line has emerged from two sources that cannot be suppressed: the army and the party theoretical institute, both of which have major publications and influence over media and organizations and can express themselves relatively freely in public. Together, they represent by far the most powerful opposition that the party has ever confronted in its entire history, and their very existence reflects the reality that while the Politburo has discouraged and sometimes suppressed dissenters within its own ranks, the crisis within the party has generated profound disagreements which neither the majority nor the critical minority can resolve. Both sides' arguments have been on an abysmally low level and reflect the pervasive analytic and theoretical underdevelopment that suffuses the entire party. The dilemma is that while the powerful critics of the market know precisely what they are against, they have failed to employ the most effective economic case for their own side. More important, they are pathetically devoid of viable alternatives, and this fact alone may result in the present policies continuing by default.

Nonetheless, while the entire party nominally deplores "pluralism," it is itself now practicing it. The factions share a consensus only on the party retaining total power, but since they cannot agree on the means for attaining socialism, or how to define it in institutional terms, profound disagreements exist within its ranks. In reality, an increasingly serious stalemate has emerged.

As a result of the army's and others' growing alienation, an astonishing amount of information on corruption, social unrest, strikes, food problems, the creation of a class society, and much else, has been published; most of the critical information in this book comes from official sources. The Vietnamese press is much more iconoclastic and irreverent toward its society's conventional wisdom and institutions than most, if not all, major American or European publications. Nothing like it ever existed in the USSR or China, and while the party deplores a theory formally justifying such press freedom as "pluralism" or "peaceful evolution," a remarkably open press nonetheless functions today. In this context, the pessimistic political conclusions that critics are drawing are far more daring than anything that has ever appeared in Communist Vietnam's history.

The army's increasingly independent role is partially the result of the party's effort since the end of the war to redefine its role. In 1984, General Van Tien Dung, the army's head and a technocrat who had little patience with ideology, abolished the decisive post of the independent political commissar in the army, fundamentally shifting its command structure. He thereby infuriated many senior officers with deep political convictions, and in December 1986 they had him removed in disgrace from the Politburo. There was nothing in the army's past that hinted they might challenge civilian authority, but *doi moi* severely tried them all personally. Apart from the way it neglected millions of veterans and their families, reform ruthlessly cut military pay to well below that of production and administrative workers. Career officers' pensions, in particular, were gutted, compelling many of them to remain beyond their twenty-five-year service obligation. Some were faced with up to fifteen or more years of additional duty. If anything could arouse their opposition, this was it. While it always alluded to instability in the rest of the Communist world, the menace of "peaceful evolution" was always identified with the longstanding efforts to "depoliticise" the army, and in September 1992 the political cadres were reinstated to their crucial position.[15] It also made it clear that to protect the nation's territorial integrity the army had also to defend "the socialist system" at home, including the "infrastructure . . . of socialism."[16] It never defined precisely what this might involve or who its enemies were. Whatever its other motives since then, which as much as any single factor unquestionably reflect their very real, deep ideological convictions, from the inception the reform's impact compelled the army officers to guard their institutional interests; however vague or even paranoid its rhetoric, there is also a material basis for it. By forcing the army into this position, it was inevitable that the divisions that emerged within the party after 1994 would cause it to align itself with those who still took socialism seriously. The army, for the first time, became a major political player.

In mid-1994 the army daily newspaper, in a scathing attack which had no precedent, deplored the widespread party "bureaucratism, authoritarianism," and corruption and expressed fear that the party could "eventually disintegrate, as experienced by parties in many countries." It was imperative "to restore the people's trust in the party and state" lest it "lead to the danger of losing the party's leadership and the collapse of the regime." Rebuking prevailing methods, it demanded that "we must promote true democracy" and insisted "that the principle of democratic centralism has not been seriously and correctly implemented" – all the while demanding the need for "firm discipline."[17] The army, more than any other sector within the party, began to oppose the majority consensus.

Since then the army has gone to major lengths to facilitate "strengthening the political capabilities of officers in accord with the position of the working class," implying that there is a limit to the extent it can be relied upon should Vietnam pursue the logic of its present course and abandon socialism.[18] About this time it also "institutionalized" its "coordination" with the equally unhappy interior ministry – the police – "with a clear division of functions and duties."[19] Ideological screening and indoctrination within its own ranks have increased greatly. The army's sustained harsh criticisms of the dominant party line have been cast in an ambiguous manner that reflects both its profound discontent and endemic intellectual confusion. Until the end of 1995 it made continuous obscure references to "peaceful evolution" plots (a phrase borrowed from the Chinese), subversion, and nameless enemies both within and outside the country, including those who have "infiltrated into the party." More important, it stood resolutely against the dominant "pragmatism, commercialism, [and] extreme individualism" inherent in market socialism.[20]

The market throws down the gauntlet

By mid-1995, the possibility of a crisis between the two fundamentally opposing sides began to increase significantly, not least because Vo Van Kiet in August 1995 raised the stakes and obtained the Politburo's approval for a comprehensive reorganization of the entire government administration – which he, more than anyone else, runs – to insulate it from arbitrary party control and create a nominally rationalized legal system that could institutionalize the market economy: "build a legal system suitable to the market-oriented mechanism and to the direction of socialism," as it was later described.[21] This change was intended eventually to restructure the entire state economy. Both the IMF and World Bank had long pressed for such revisions, their future aid was always contingent explicitly on reforms like it, and Kiet freely used many of their arguments as his own. But this ambitious project was vague in many crucial regards, and very discretionary – indeed, it would essentially replace the role of the party in the state administration with a no less predictable group of nonelected bureaucrats unresponsive to any needs save their own. It was far more a wish list than an articulate plan; only its general direction was unmistakable. It would certainly make Kiet primus inter pares and in control of a huge patronage network. The party would be seriously marginalized institutionally, a process that is already well along in fact if not theory. Instability of any sort was alone a severe threat to the market-caucus centered around Kiet and the huge constituency benefiting from the transition. They wanted finally to settle the institutional question and move forward.

It is first necessary to position the IMF and World Bank in this evolving confrontation. Both, as I mentioned earlier, have been major participants in what the Bank described as "a policy dialogue with the Government since the late 1980s," but it was not until late 1993 that the United States allowed the Bank to resume financial aid. In May 1994 the Bank established an office in Hanoi and proceeded to "provide advice" on all the legal and technical steps essential for "the transition to a market economy" and by 1996 nearly a hundred Bank and IMF experts were working on or in Vietnam.[22] The Bank's role was directly linked to Vietnam's dealings with the IMF and its commercial debt restructuring: in effect, to its ability to expand into the international economy. Most World Bank loans are everywhere in the world "coordinated with the IMF's overall economic program for the country."[23] Even more crucial, in 1993 various nations and international banks pledged Vietnam $1.8 billion in largely "soft" loans (but also some non-refundable aid) and $2 billion in 1994. For these sums actually to be committed and then disbursed, however, Vietnam had first to meet a series of strict conditions, some of which were purely technical, but they were contingent mainly on implementing the legal and administrative changes the IMF and World Bank defined, for much of the money was filtered through it.[24] By July 1996 only one-third had been committed to specific projects but a mere 5 percent had been actually disbursed.[25] In return for paltry IMF loans, Vietnam had responded eagerly to their bait and advice since 1988, and now a huge and tempting promise was dangling before it.

When the two institutions referred to legality, however, they had no intention whatsoever of empowering the people, and there was no concept whatsoever of autonomous justice involved. Law meant institutionalizing the market and equality for all investors, foreign and local. The World Bank used Vietnam's future access to this growing, undisbursed foreign aid reserve as the incentive for its accepting a strictly economic definition of law. After years of sustained contact with the government, the Bank had every reason to believe that it could work through the maze of Vietnamese politics to gain its prize, which is the same everywhere: abolishing socialism.

Kiet's bloc moved quickly to begin implementing the ambitious administrative plan, and in October 1995 the National Assembly voted for a comprehensive civil code that legally enshrined property rights in a manner superseding in practice the party's vague socialist declarations. In the first of a long series of steps, eight ministries were compressed into three. "The reshuffle," one Vietnamese source observed, "ended the Stalinist-style administrative structure and signified our move toward a more westernized system."[26] But rather than reduce the bureaucracy, which would only earn him enemies, Kiet created a large number of new general corporations, presumably modelled on the South Korean state-sponsored economic conglomerates but with no clear economic responsibilities. If anything, the changes added significantly to the existing administrative confusion. No one was fired; instead, "some people who previously served as ministers or vice ministers are now chairmen of the board – that is, they are businessmen."[27] This illusory reform merely allows the market advocates to extend their power base and by no means alters the state's arbitrary nature or corruption; if anything, it increases it. Legality was only a contrived excuse for shifting the locus of power away from the party and to the government machinery, concentrated in Kiet's office, neither of which are in any way responsible to the people.

The IMF and the World Bank were fully aware of this emerging confrontation, and they were entirely candid about their relation to it. Apart from the undisbursed aid they controlled, Vietnam's foreign debt, already very high by the standards of poor nations, demands a restructuring that would also compel it to accept stringent conditions if it hopes to obtain greater access to the international capital market. Because its large, rapidly growing trade deficit requires it to borrow or sharply reduce its imports – and growth – loans are becoming all the more imperative. But Vietnam in the fall of 1995 had first to restructure its already existing foreign commercial debt, and it could not do so unless the IMF and the World Bank approved its economic policies. They would do so only if Vietnam, as with every nation, conformed to its strict conditions on structural adjustments, which affect fundamentally its entire economic strategy.

The IMF and the World Bank have never made the slightest secret of their intentions, and they understood fully how they were aiding Kiet's alliance politically and intimidating his critics. From the fall of 1995 to mid-1996, both institutions provided the market advocates with enormous leverage. To let it be known how powerful they were, Kiet's forces blatantly, even provocatively, flouted their intimate connections with the two institutions. In November 1995, when a joint IMF–World Bank delegation came to Hanoi with comprehensive advice for the entire economy, this relationship was openly highly political and dealt directly with the most fundamental economic policies. Later that month, prior to a meeting of donors in Paris to deal with aid to Vietnam, the director and staff of the World Bank's Vietnam department met journalists in London and discussed the major policy debate within the party; the Bank was disturbed by the socialists' efforts to reserve a larger role for the public sector, to prevent privatization, and the like. Policy making was stalled until the congress; the Bank "can only advise the government." Paris would allow the donors "to communicate their views."[28] The Bank was very much a part of the emerging crisis within the party; indeed, it was also one of its major causes.

By December 1995 Vietnam had earned very high marks by IMF and World Bank standards, for they knew that the reformers were well on their way to abandoning socialism in practice while retaining it in name only. To have deserted them at this point would have greatly strengthened their enemies; in a word, if Vietnam was deeply in the debt trap, the IMF was also ensnared by the imminent opportunity to incorporate one of the few remaining Communist nations into the global capitalist economy. The Vietnamese delegation to the Paris meeting brought with it the framework of the five-year plan to be presented to the June 1996 congress, and the donors from twenty nations and sixteen international organizations discussed it with them and "endorsed" it.[29] The donors made it crystal clear that enlarging the private sector was their top priority. They also committed themselves to $2.3 billion in new aid in 1996, about four-fifths in soft loans. With this huge backing, Kiet and his allies could look forward to the congress with equanimity, assuming that the lure of money would overcome their opponents. They were so confident they could intimidate them that their own press release on the meeting repeated details of the crucial policy accord verbatim from the World Bank's statement.[30]

Although the IMF complained to the Vietnamese about "some delays occurring in several important areas," the Vietnamese convinced them that they "are moving forward with a wide range of structural reforms."[31] As a proof, in February 1996 the IMF loaned Vietnam $178 million, including the usual structural obligations; they were to be implemented or Vietnam could not obtain the commercial loans it required. More important, it had first to settle with its existing commercial debtors. The IMF's imprimatur made that possible.

But to make certain the party stays its course, the president of the World Bank himself, James Wolfensohn, visited Hanoi in early May and offered ample advice on how it should do so, explicitly endorsing the legal reforms that Kiet was implementing. He also offered Vietnam $1.5 billion in credits over a three-year period with the inevitable conditions on favoring the private sector, but he made it explicit that the forthcoming congress had also to play its part:

> I came away with the sense from the economic leadership that they are anxious to create an environment for investment and that . . . as soon as they can achieve this harmony – and I guess you will see this discussed at the next congress – we can expect an environment in which Vietnam will move ahead.[32]

"If we look back at the origin of this country . . .," he commented with supreme understatement, the changes "in recent times are remarkable."[33] To add to the bait, a few days later Vietnam's private creditors also played their crucial part and agreed to renegotiate $900 million in commercial arrears at ostensibly extremely favorable terms that "surprised" many bankers, promising to forgive close to half of it.[34] Once the deal was signed, Vietnam could resume borrowing in the international capital market.

Altogether, the package of promised loans and grants from December 1995 until the congress alone amounted to about $3.5 billion, and most of the previously committed $3.8 had yet to be spent. This cornucopia, huge by Vietnam's standards, is entirely dependent on its adhering to strict conditions, and it can be disbursed only in tranches as they are met. But the IMF and the Bank had very boldly but generously flexed their astonishing financial muscle, and they sought overtly to tempt the party congress. In reality, they were attempting to buy it. But they then went one step further.

Advocates of socialism, especially the army, had for some time been demanding that the state sector must "fulfill its leading role," with "more concentration" on its direction of the economy.[35] This issue increasingly became the focus of their differences with the market advocates. During the first months of 1996, they urged that 60 percent of the GDP be the goal for the state economy in 2020. Since the present figure is about 37 percent, this would require a great deal more state ownership than at present: in effect, a total policy reversal. Sixty percent became a crucial symbol, but the reformers wanted no inhibiting reference to numbers in the congress's report. While the World Bank delegation was in Hanoi it was asked for its wholly predictable opinion, and it was, according to a journalist's account, "sharply critical of the target."[36] Armed with this mandate, with billions of dollars at stake, the reformers managed to get all numerical goals excluded from the congress document.

Kiet and his allies had played a very powerful but brutal card, for it involved open foreign interference, and they must have been desperate to do so. Could the army allow the IMF and the World Bank, avowed enemies of socialism, to define Vietnam's very future, or accept defeat under these circumstances? The lines between the two sides had never been so stark – or provocative.

*

It was in this increasingly charged atmosphere that toward the end of 1995, for the first time since the Communists came to power, rumors circulated in Hanoi that the army was reaching the limits of its patience and might become much more, even openly, aggressive. "The internal contradictions inside the party are becoming more acute," an informed party member told a reporter a few months later. "The battle will get worse."[37] The army's public statements from this time until the June 1996 party congress certainly added credibility to these threats. At the end of 1995 it began for the first time to identify the "market economy" explicitly as the principal threat to socialism, and even implied that its advocates within the party were objectively pursuing the goals of American imperialists who still believe that implementing the market line is a decisive precondition for "the final victory – the victory in peace – [that] will belong to the United States."[38] It also took direct aim at Kiet's administrative plan for "a law-governed state to distance itself from the class viewpoint . . . the danger posed by opportunistic and rightist elements is more serious than ever before."[39]

For the next half-year it continued to focus on "the seamy side of the market economy"; in early June 1996, its daily paper deplored an alleged plot by Vietnamese exiles to drive a wedge between the army and the party, which only served to remind the party that such a split indeed might exist.[40] As if to confirm it, the day after this article appeared an official army "commentator" issued a widely circulated attack that went beyond all previous criticism. He reiterated the earlier theme that the army's mandate includes not just the defense of Vietnam's territorial integrity but also of "Marxism-Leninism and Ho Chi Minh Thought," toward which "some people in the contingent of our cadres, party members, and people have shown their vacillating and suspicious attitude. . . ." To defeat the peaceful evolution "strategy to eliminate socialism," all sorts of rectifications had to be made: "first of all, the errors made by the internal organization; neutralize the opposition of bad elements inside; and crush the dark schemes of outside forces." For the first time, these foreign enemies explicitly included the IMF, the World Bank, and the Asian Development Bank, whose "conditions do not have a purely economic character only" and who sought to "liberate the remaining socialist countries through privatization and free market." It deplored the casinos and golf courses the market-advocates were creating. "In whatever war, the main force that confronts the enemy is the national defense force," and this task included "subversive activities."[41]

By naming the international banks and alluding to its partisans within the party as enemies, the army went further than it had ever done. A few days before the congress, a Bangkok daily newspaper quoted a seasoned diplomat in Hanoi that the military, supported by the Interior Ministry in charge of the police, wanted "some real power," and would assert its strength.[42] One key to its success was the role that General Le Kha Phieu, the army's chief political commissar and a Politburo member, would play in the Politburo about to be chosen. As if to confirm this point and reiterate its position over the preceding year, the day before the congress opened the army daily paper issued a long unsigned statement reflecting its official view: it had the central role in maintaining not only territorial integrity but "political stability" in the face of the challenge of "peaceful evolution." This plot included the attempt to dilute "the idealist goal of socialism," which it repeatedly defined in its classic form without any of the modifications and contingencies which had been employed during a decade of *doi moi* to obfuscate and transform the concept.[43] The word "market" was not used once. The market was now the explicit enemy.

The army had unmistakably flexed its muscles, thereby identifying itself as the principal institutional rival to the policies that the IMF and the World Bank had so successfully sponsored; it stood as the only other potentially serious player insofar as power, as opposed to rhetoric, is concerned. Whatever else occurred, this split revealed that the Communist party's traditional, private, consensual way of operating had finally ended; how it would rule in the future was cast into grave doubt.

To this extent, the army had by June 1996 articulated a distinctive ideological stance on key socioeconomic issues, if only by reasserting one that had been discarded. While its belief in discipline seemed most likely to prove stronger, the military's potential to play an independent role in the future had to be considered very seriously – by the Politburo and the entire central committee. The question was: Would they do so and, if so, what would this entail?

*

Although no other force possesses anything like the army's power, by the spring of 1996 there were other elements within the party, both formal and informal, who either objectively or intentionally reinforced its position. The most visible of these, but not necessarily the most important, was the party theoretical institute, the keeper of the official faith, headed by Nguyen Duc Binh, a senior Politburo member.

The party institute's dilemma reflects partially the fact that events have compelled it to attempt to adapt theory to reality – and it has been unable to do so. So long as there was a war, its tasks were easy to define and involved few real choices, and theory could exist in cosmic isolation, asserting comfortingly that laws predestined human history and that Communists had been assigned the role as inevitable victors – and everything they did was only a necessary step in that ineluctable process. By the mid-1980s, when a great deal of wisdom and knowledge of events in the world was required, the official doctrine consisted of ritual declarations of faith but it had no analytic utility whatsoever when it came to comprehending the market line, much less resisting it. The whole complex world had simply bypassed its nineteenth-century ideological framework. The entire debate that occurred after *doi moi* was inaugurated rarely referred to the dire experiences in other developing nations which had applied the IMF's and the World Bank's strictures. Practical men like Kiet have no interest whatsoever in ideas but only in results as expressed in growth rates. The theoretical institute, like the oracles of Delphi, is revered but also ignored, and it is being marginalized. As experience revealed the market line's enormous, debilitating consequences, the theoreticians began increasingly to align themselves in unequivocal terms against the majority "market" line; its widely read, authoritative journal has published the ablest critiques of it – many of which I have used here. Writers in it have graphically described the party's deplorable morale and corruption and stated plainly that "If the leadership of the party and the control of the state don't go to the heart of these negative factors, it will be difficult to maintain political stability in the face of the strength of money . . . we will be committing suicide."[44] But while the institute still has immense prestige, if only because theory is still venerated by many, it has no institutional base: no clients indebted to it, material objects to distribute, or those assets that count most in an increasingly worldly nation. Nonetheless, ideological authority and correctness is something the army desperately needs.

There were other, even more prestigious, leaders by the spring of 1996 who were prepared to reinforce the army's general critique, not so much by formally collaborating with it but by sharing, and thereby fortifying, its reluctance to abandon socialism in deed if not word. By then it was undeniable that an uninhibited frontier capitalism based on blatant inequality was corrupting not only the youth but many party members, and cynicism and cultural pollution were rampant. Many of the sincere idealists who had most favored *doi moi* at its inception now conceded that its negative social consequences were both enormous and painful; and while few wanted to return to the earlier strategy they hesitated to continue with the market – most, indeed, hoped for an alternative to both the market and a command economy, which none of them had the sensitivity or ability to outline. To frame such a new option, indeed, required breaking radically with the consensual, ineffective way the leaders had always resolved their problems, and that would entail a sharp break. It was this mode of operating which had allowed the nation to drift into the abyss.

Nguyen Van Linh, the nominal architect of *doi moi*, was by far the most vociferous and important member of this group – he was publicly horrified by his inspiration's results. He was especially hostile toward Kiet, once his closest ally, whom he publicly accused of corruption via his wife, who flaunts her great wealth openly.[45] But there were innumerable others; privately, many senior as well as ordinary members let it be known that they felt the market had escaped control and they were extremely unhappy about it.

These are all deeply sincere and honest men and women. For the most part, they are simply bewildered by events; they do not quite comprehend what went wrong, much less how they were directly responsible for it, but it was now undeniable that the party was failing – probably fatally. They no longer gave the market carte blanche. Publicly, even normally docile senior leaders from the Fatherland Front also issued dire warnings: "The current corruption is a national disaster and an internal rebellion that will undermine our nation's security each passing day."[46] And apart from these tendencies, countless lower-ranking, mainly older party veterans now felt alienated by the results of their life's work.

In essence, notwithstanding their ritual proclamations that unity prevails, the party by 1996 was profoundly divided on fundamental issues that will define the very fate of socialism.

All this strengthened the army's ability to advance its position, not so much in the belief that it would gain active supporters but that a very great deal of possible opposition to it had disappeared. Its basic problem is that it has no mass or social base outside its own ranks and it has not shown the slightest inclination to build one among the countless peasants or the exploited urban workers who are the natural constituencies for a return to socialist objectives. It never refers to the "mass line" because the army fears intensely some vague, indefinite specter called "pluralism." It cannot build alliances with the people, who would have to be endowed with authority, and it does not see power as a product of real politics. Fundamentally, it would like to issue orders and have them obeyed. Officers are used to commanding and therefore they are not essentially political, even in the authoritarian populist sense quite common in the Third World. Having no sense of the dynamics of power or classes within society and what they must do to utilize it, the army's sincere commitment to socialism is not likely to cause it to make those strategic political concessions essential to attaining it. In the end, if compelled to choose between socialism without absolute order or the growing evils of the market with it, it is much more likely to opt for the latter – if only by default.

But the ultimate inhibition on the army at this point is that, regardless of how it obtains power or on what conditions, it does not know what to do with it. It is absolutely clear in its own mind what it is opposed to but it is incapable of defining socialism programmatically – in a word, in terms of what it favors. Although it was never in a position before mid-1996 that required it to do so, and because the mere searching for alternatives to the existing party line was always deemed a lack of discipline, the army failed to prepare itself for the enormous responsibility it says it must finally be prepared to assume. It is, in the last analysis, an army, however brilliant militarily, that has precious few ideas as to how really to defend socialism. Faith, or its noble devotion, is hardly sufficient. The army does not realize, even though it declares itself political, that social problems and specific institutional decisions cannot be solved simply by giving orders. The only effective defense of socialism is to make it work better than its alternatives, and specific programs are mandatory. An immense amount of critical, serious effort is required, and it had to begin much earlier; it lost a great deal of essential time, and time always favors the status quo everywhere. For this reason, those whom it criticizes did not take it very seriously. The army is potentially a great inconvenience but they felt quite confident they could convince it not to destabilize an increasingly structured capitalism pretending to be an ideologically neutral economy. Indeed, they could show it quite convincingly that were it to take power without a credible alternative it might easily create chaos.

Still, the real question by mid-1996 was not whether the army and its allies could guide the nation successfully back to socialism but whether this informal coalition was ready to block Kiet's alliance. That, in itself, would be the harbinger of a fundamental crisis within the Communist party – the first, indeed, in its entire history. Were they to do so, the possibilities for Vietnam's future might change a very great deal – notwithstanding the IMF's confidence that it was already "irreversible."[47] Since time immemorial, politics has always defined the ultimate parameters within which economies function, and Vietnam's case will be no different.

The congress

From the viewpoint of rhetoric, it was no more likely that this congress would be any more explicit about basic economic policies than previous congresses have been. The party's natural divisions and real confusion, which have enabled the IMF to fill its analytic vacuum so easily since 1986, make abstraction and contradiction the rule rather than the exception. One could invariably read very different things into most of its statements. The draft political report it released in April 1996 confirmed the party's inability to formulate a clear, unequivocal program – and it remained virtually unchanged in June. Its socioeconomic report, on the other hand, had the usual socialist rhetoric but it was characteristically vague; however, its specifics tilted heavily in favor of Kiet's administrative restructuring. The absence of any percentage fixed as a target for the state's share of the economy meant very little, save insofar as Kiet's alliance and the World Bank asked that none be set. The compromise reached was not incompatible with a higher or lower state role. As always, a characteristic opaqueness suffused the party's general program. Far more significant was who would obtain the key slots in the Politburo and dominate the structure of organizational power. They alone could hope to define events. This reality created every incentive to obtaining control of the Politburo.

At the beginning of 1996 the Politburo leaders – whose average age is 71 – had publicly discussed stepping down and allowing much younger and technically qualified men to take over. But as time wore on it was clear that the increasing infighting and differences dividing the party were much too great, and that political loyalty was far more crucial than competence. At the end of April the struggle became unprecedentedly brutal when Nguyen Ha Phan, one of the lesser Politburo members allied with the antimarket group, was expelled from both the Politburo and even the party for allegedly having betrayed his comrades during the war. It is unlikely that this charge was true, but it was virtually certain that, even if it were, it had not just come to light at this opportune moment. Nothing remotely like it had ever occurred, but a few weeks later, a Politburo member ranking eleventh on the seventeen-member body, a likely ally of the antimarket side, was compelled to resign for corruption – a charge that may have been true but also was unquestionably not new. Besides, once corruption is used as a criterion there are others also guilty of some form of it, especially among the market advocates. In effect, the reformers began to fight dangerously and with all available means. Intrigue and rumors were rife. They certainly could have expected a response.

According to the party's constitution, the central committee is nominally its ruling body between its five-year congresses. It was in this mood of growing tension that the 160-odd members of the central committee met for an unprecedented three extended sessions during May and June in a grueling, sustained secret debate. Two members (one of whom, Le Mai, I knew well for twenty-five years) died of heart attacks. Others fell seriously ill. The party's platform itself could not have caused such a crisis, because it has always been contradictory or ambiguous enough to satisfy everybody, and it was this time also. Speculation as to who would replace the existing Politburo, and especially its top members, was rife. Something, clearly, was very wrong, and it involved much more than the usual regional demands for power or the traditional patronage problems.

In the past, the Politburo's ranking personalities, at the most five or six among the seventeen, effectively shaped policy, but lesser members also frequently asserted themselves and, in the last analysis, according to the party constitution their votes are equal. All members are potentially in a position to play a significant role. This informal arrangement worked so long as the possibility of a consensus existed, for which a basis could always be found either through vague resolutions, which were almost the rule, or through patronage. This informal method unified the party successfully for a half-century and spared it the terrible purges that wracked the other Communist states. Its de facto inequality did not need to be institutionalized, and any effort to do so might fundamentally alter the way the Communist party has operated until now. Only an unprecedented crisis, therefore, could lead to its being made an explicit rule. That moment had arrived. The struggle within the party in the period before the congress involved the very future of the party, and certainly of socialism.

Here a seemingly minor background issue must be introduced. In late January 1996, a draft revision of the party statutes was circulated publicly; it was essentially a complex and convoluted revision of the Politburo's structure, the rationale for which at this time seemed unclear but not necessarily important.[48] A standing board was to be created within the Politburo and it would be assigned control over the entire party's work, merely formalizing the practice of preceding decades. But the Politburo *or* its new standing board was also to supervise the central committee's crucial military commission, while the standing board would supervise the army political general department also. Where this left those Politburo members not on the standing board was unclear, for the alterations explicitly concentrated a great deal more administrative power in the hands of a few men. This change seemed relatively benign because the central committee was to elect the standing bureau members as well as the Politburo's other members. This check alone prevented what would otherwise seem a decisive shift in the control of the entire party structure, the Politburo, and, above all, the army. Had it been only this that the central committee was asked to approve, it would have done so easily because it did not infringe basically its role; it was adminis-trative, not substantive. But an undisclosed issue had wracked the central committee's June meetings; something had changed, and it was potentially very important. It was almost certainly this proposal.

Party congresses have traditionally been rubber stamps, their participants highly reliable; in this case, over four-fifths of the 1,200 delegates were functionaries, and when it met at the end of June the Politburo was so certain it would perform on cue that it allowed the entire proceedings to be televised for the first time. All went well until the final day, when it was time to vote on changes in the party statutes; a delegate stood up from the floor and electrified the hall by objecting to the creation of a proposed standing board within the Politburo and detailing to the entire nation exactly how profound the complex technical revision was. The Politburo itself rather than the central committee would appoint the board. A fundamental change had been made in the original amendment! The board would have the right to make decisions on behalf of the Politburo, annexing much of its power and remaining independent of the central committee's ultimate control. The thoroughly prepared critic confronted both Do Muoi and President Le Duc Anh in a detailed and direct discussion, and they defensively employed sleights of hand to insist that the standing committee's specific mandate would come from the Politburo; it would only act on its behalf. But the audacious delegate revealed that there were nineteen major responsibilities transferred directly to it – in effect, its position was at the top of the party hierarchy and largely autonomous of it. His proposal to abolish the standing board was swept aside – but he was widely applauded.[49] The congress members, like the entire party, were deeply divided.

In fact, while there is a certain vagueness in the standing board's general authority, which only experience over time can clarify, it is due largely to the great ambiguity regarding the functions of the remainder of the Politburo, which is now marginalized institutionally. That too must be resolved, and in the interim the decision-making power will be redefined at a time when it can least afford to be. What is certain is that the change is intended to insulate the military commission and the army political general department from everyone but the standing board, and that anything either does in the future with its agreement is legal! It also protects the army from any effort, which inevitably will come as Kiet's reorganization advances, to depoliticize it and eliminate it as a political force, and the new arrangement could be as much defensive as offensive. But to open a fundamental, inherently destabilizing debate on such issues at this crucial moment was scarcely a casual decision. It certainly was not done for adminis-trative efficiency; in fact, it makes all the greater the likelihood of each side attempting to outflank the other by whatever means possible. In any struggle for the control of the levers of power, the state bureaucracy under Kiet is far better placed to win than anyone. It is too soon to define the standing board's role clearly. It certainly was not by itself a palace coup but its power could be very great, perhaps decisive, for those prepared to make it so. The intentions of those who maneuvered the change became much clearer when the standing board's membership was announced.

The five members designated to the standing board were Do Muoi, the party secretary-general, President Le Duc Anh, a mild-mannered former officer and critic of the market, and Prime Minister Vo Van Kiet, the principal architect of the market revolution since its inception. Le Kha Phieu, the army's chief political commissar, came next, and the Politburo's nominally lowest-ranking member, Nguyen Tan Dung, was fifth. Dung was vice minister of interior – the police – and an ally of Phieu. Since Do Muoi tacks with the prevailing political winds, the antimarket forces are certainly preponderant on the standing board. Six of the eighteen Politburo members are from the army or police, although several others tend to agree with them on economic questions, and only four are clearly identified with the market. At least for the moment, *doi moi*'s enemies, with the army in the leadership, have carried the day. The ultimate question is whether the remainder of the party and nation will obey the board any more than it had the preceding Politburo. What else can it do to impose its real authority? Only time will tell.

Apart from this one change, the party congress resolved nothing because the leaders are now irrevocably divided and they will continue their conflict in other ways, the intensity of which cannot be predicted. But all the real issues remain the same. Even before the congress ended, there was talk of more conferences to attempt to resolve the obdurate issues – perhaps in 1998 if not earlier. Then, it was said, the top three leaders may be able to step down – if alternatives can be agreed upon – and this prospect may reduce tension. Meanwhile, each faction will try to mobilize its power in local party organizations, and insofar as discipline ceases to constrain members or there are those who still care enough, a surrogate democracy might even emerge within its ranks, for two distinctly different parties now exist. But the indecisive struggle will continue for better or worse, with the increasingly powerful state administration extending its organizational role, and in the process socialism's lingering institutional residues are most likely to be eroded even further. Time favors all those who would abolish it: the cynical bureaucrats and corruptionists who run the government, those who are amassing their fortunes, and the IMF and the World Bank.

Vietnam will then go the way of the other Communist nations.

Conclusion

Winning the war and losing the peace

The Vietnamese Communist party was unable to find its way when it achieved its coveted victory because a political structure that was adapted admirably for war became counterproductive the moment it ended. Leninist parties from their very inception were everywhere organized to confront repression and war, and their astonishing triumph in so many nations only reinforced their conviction that their essentially militarized structure would prove equally successful in peace. But communism as a major phase in modern world history, at least in its original socialist form, has now virtually disappeared. This reality has cast an oppressive shadow over the Vietnamese party. The overwhelming burden of proof is now upon it; it must transcend a modern historical experience which has spared very few nations that began as Communist. Until now it has steadily been failing what is very probably its last opportunity to survive – its final battle in a struggle that has endured a half-century.

Vietnam's difficult and unstable trajectory since 1987 has created many people who have benefited materially, upon whom the government and the media focus almost exclusively, but there have also been innumerable losers, and these increasingly abandoned people are precisely those who sacrificed the most to make the revolution secure. They cannot and may refuse to be discounted. Whatever economic achievements Vietnam has attained until now are fragile, both because most of these gains are intrinsically very vulnerable and, above all, because there has not been comparable political, cultural, and social progress. On the contrary! As in war, where the struggle had to be fought on many fronts, peace had to produce success in all of the nation's decisive social and economic institutions, this time for the large majority. The party will not endure otherwise.

The Communist leaders now proclaim the same total faith in the market mythology that once they devoted to dialectical materialism or to Soviet models which they later confessed were not suited to Vietnamese conditions. But they are astonishingly ignorant of economic realities and experiences elsewhere, and they lack elementary information concerning topics on which they have made crucial decisions. Worst of all, they have become increasingly immune to the ethical and social values and goals that ultimately determine policy choices. Their simplistic notions of the accumulation process ignore the concept of total capital, which stresses the long-term importance of a trained and healthy population, and they have allowed the so-called market to be implemented in a promiscuous manner that is emptying the socialist ideal of its human content and meaning. The party leaders are mainly shrewd political operators within their own closed, self-sufficient world, and they have been unable to guide the nation successfully through the complex shoals of reconstruction. Vo Van Kiet and his allies use ideologies, whether called market or socialist, merely as pragmatic tools to advance their strategic objectives and power. As with Russia's rulers today, they are consummate cynics.

The party's definitions of economics now comprise directly contradictory rhetoric taken from both socialist and capitalist doctrines. This inherently unstable synthesis cannot obscure the increasingly unequal ownership of wealth and the control of property, or the new economic elite that has emerged – as in Russia and China – largely out of the party itself. As in both those nations, "market" theory is only a façade to justify their sustained confiscation of wealth. The only real coherence in their thinking is in their desire to retain power, first under communism and then under its successor, whether it is called capitalism, as in Russia, or socialism, as in China and Vietnam. The system that is emerging is really neither of these systems, but rather a historically unprecedented hybrid synthesis of the worst aspects of both of them, specific only to the Communist nations during their final stages of disintegration.

There was no "objective" strategy or painless course open to the Communists after 1975, but only a choice between options that reflected the intensity of their commitment to those social goals and priorities inherent in the very concept of socialism, funda-mental values that demarcate all basic ideologies. Rather than make these difficult decisions, in part to maintain unity within its own ranks but also because it was not prepared to do so wisely, the Politburo abandoned the vast responsibility inherent in its absolute authority with the excuse that the allegedly necessitarian "laws of economics" would inevitably spare it the trouble, and history would end in the party's favor. It is not doing so.

A great deal of creative thought was mandatory, and clarity without its misleading heritage of rhetoric and fixations had to inform their debates. This intellectual rigor had to be applied constantly and critically and, above all, the core commitments that provide socialism with its very raison d'être had to inspire it. Given the Politburo's assertion that its mastery of absolute truth justified its monopoly on power, at no time was it open to those new ideas or that information essential to achieving its socialist objectives. It has never dared to compare its claim to infallibility with its repeated past failures as well as successes, and its defeats after 1975 were just as frequent as its triumphs before then. But the war was over, the Politburo's decisive role no longer suited the nation's increasingly complex needs, and it failed to transcend the war's lessons; its ineffectiveness thereby threatened to under-mine the victory that had been won at a monumental cost to the people.

The result was persistent, endemic drift, with occasional but futile efforts to undo the inevitable damage. Socialism's basic goals were first postponed, then increasingly forgotten. By the mid-1990s the party could no longer offer a coherent, meaningful definition of them, and it relied increasingly on ritual clichés. Its primary objective was to keep itself in power when in fact its actions were certain to erode gravely its moral prestige – and eventually its mastery. The only inevitability in such a refusal to lead, when no one else had the capacity to do so, is failure.

The illusions of "efficiency" inspiring them, and the intellectu-ally scandalous assertion that new "objective laws" were dis-covered – in reality under IMF and technocratic direction – is just one more convincing reason why Vietnam's present leaders should leave the future to the guidance of others and to truly democratic institutions. Given the diversity and enormity of the responsibilities a long war created, their fixation on growth rates as the decisive criterion of success is comparable to the U.S.

obsession with body counts during the war it lost. When peace came, the party forgot the logic of its philosophy of war; the political, ideological, and social challenges crucial to comprehensive reconstruction were, at the most, assigned secondary importance. It was confident that its very existence would guarantee its future control and social stability. It has not.

The Politburo's determination to concentrate final power in its own hands made a political crisis within the party inevitable, because it is inherently impossible to govern a nation as large and diverse as Vietnam in a highly centralized manner. But the Politburo denied this reality and, rather than adapt to it and impose some minimum, practical national standards, thereby made it mandatory for each province and agency of government to adapt accordingly. By striving for absolute control, it achieved far less than it might have done. The provincial political and administrative structure has therefore become increasingly autonomous, creating a fundamental challenge to the Politburo's authority.

Even more important, the very nature of the Politburo makes it impossible for it to govern. From its inception it was always a consensual body, reducing policies to the lowest common denominator, and this has increasingly left decisions with local parties. Since 1993 it has been profoundly divided. Indeed, it is united basically only in its desire to retain absolute power, but scarcely more. It is comprised of a minority distinctly favoring socialism, but incapable of translating it into meaningful institutional alternatives, and another minority of reformers who wish to create a "market" economy. Whatever the so-called reformers' pretensions, they have been the only group since 1986 that has made specific proposals for every problem. Mainly in charge of the government, they are systematically introducing values and institutions that are destroying the organizational residues of socialism, above all in the land system, which will define the shape of the new economy decisively. Their precise equivalents existed in the Soviet Union during its final years. Employing the same vision, Deng Xiaoping radically transformed China. The balance of power in the Politburo until mid-1996 was always in the hands of a number of congenital compromisers who wished above all to preserve the façade of unity and strove to compose their differences – thereby continuing the Politburo's irresolute role and allowing the nation to drift. It remains to be seen whether the changes in it since then will make much difference, if only because they came far too late.

The Politburo manages to command but, ironically, it less and less governs. The party's members are supposed to be disciplined but a significant minority is corrupt and many more are lax – they belong because the party offers ambitious people innumerable opportunities. The provincial parties are in many cases increasingly fiefdoms that enforce their own rules. Large parts of the economy are being exploited for private gain: managers of a significant portion of the state-controlled sector are stripping assets; good health and education are reserved mainly for those who can afford it; cadres are confiscating land and alienating peasants; youth is hypnotized by motorcycles, rock music, and a tawdry consumer culture that is manipulated and commercialized; rice in a nation that is still food-poor is being exported, forcing prices up. Everywhere one looks, there are myriad problems in virtually every aspect of society.

The question is not whether the Communist party is failing to maintain itself as the dominant institutional force, which at this point is still very much open to debate, but rather whether it is succeeding by the historic criteria that socialism as a general vision of civilized human and social relations always implied. Admittedly, such an image of a society based on social responsibility and cooperation is widely dismissed in this age of cynicism and disenchantment as hopelessly naive and old-fashioned. By these standards, which they once endorsed unequivocally, the Vietnamese Communists are failing badly. Worse yet, the party no longer aspires to attain such goals, save if they are a beneficent byproduct of economic "laws" benignly spreading their blessings, as the IMF promises they are bound eventually to do.

This growing disparity between its ideas and reality allows many party members, including many senior officials, to enrich themselves and create the new economic elite that is growing directly out of the politically dominant class. While party ideologists reiterate socialism's efficacy, other members fill their pockets. Socialist doctrine coexists with capitalist practices, and while the party officially deplores pluralism in political life, it tolerates it within its own ranks in the forms of diametrically contradictory conduct. Rhetoric is uniform but practice is not, and this paradox cannot endure indefinitely as an exploitative and elitist reality overwhelms the socialist illusion. The shrinking section of the party that has not become cynical or corrupt acknowledges the existence of a grave crisis; but most of it cannot accept the need to create the formal institutional controls over abuses that are the precondition for reversing the party's decay and preventing it from reoccurring. That would require ending the party's monopoly of power. But to preserve its hegemony despite all its shortcomings, which even most of the honest party leaders prefer, will only alienate the masses further. All this is a formula for social and political disillusion and instability.

Vietnam is now drifting precariously. Given the experiences in the rest of the Communist world, it is no exaggeration to conclude that it is confronting a grave, potentially fatal crisis – perhaps its last. At the moment of its greatest trial, there is a monumental disparity between its comprehension of its responsibilities and the real test confronting it. Despite some notable exceptions, ideas and analysis languish mostly in the hands of cynical sycophants, many of whom, like their peers in the Soviet Union during its final years, do not believe a word of what they write and will abandon socialism quickly for whatever succeeds it. By demanding total discipline, the Politburo has not only greatly constrained its own ability to understand and respond to the challenges it faces but has blocked the emergence of truly dedicated thinkers who, notwithstanding their necessary unorthodoxy on many issues, still believe in socialism. The Communist party requires far more intellectual legitimacy and insight than it possesses. It cannot trust either the wisdom or the motives of a great many of those who are called upon to justify the system publicly – and that is exceedingly dangerous.

Paralleling the party's declining standing among its own members, its draconian policies – the dismantling of the social security and education system, the creation of increasingly exploitative land conditions, and its hazardous rice policy – have alienated a very large minority of the masses who are being economically and socially marginalized. It would be foolhardy for me to exaggerate the political risks to the party from its abandoning those pledges which made the people loyal to it when its very existence depended on them; the extent to which men and women in any precarious situation will respond to it can never be predicted exactly. But the party is committing serious folly by ignoring the immense gamble that its abandonment of its original supporters could entail, not the least because the army remains sympathetic to the plight of the peasants and it alone has the force adequate to control the increasing public manifestations of discontent. The same is true for urban workers, whose nominally illegal strikes go largely unhindered. If those who command the party were themselves united, such dangers would be less grave; but they are not. Mass alienation only reinforces those who oppose the market strategy, and their ability to resist the dominant policy will grow, further undermining the already divided leaders' authority. By tolerating social dissatisfaction, the army can provide it with a degree of legitimacy.

Whatever the country or context, every economic strategy entails a political price and major social risks, a constraint that the IMF, the World Bank, and bourgeois economists cannot concede. The more draconian the measures, the greater the potential number of losers in society – and the larger the danger. The majority of the Communist leaders today share this endemic myopia, which has frequently proven to be a disastrous error in nations far better able than Vietnam to absorb social shocks.

The efficacy of the Communist structure that existed until 1975 cannot be gainsaid, for it accomplished – and whether it was by its own wisdom, its enemies' follies, or both, is now irrelevant – the monumental task of winning a war against titanic odds. But the party during the war created supportive social arrangements that gave the peasants security and sustained the high morale that was absolutely crucial to victory. The party today dismisses such "voluntarism," without which it would certainly have lost the war.

After 1975 the party had to create new social and community structures which recognized that the peace required major revisions of the wartime system while retaining its very tangible benefits for the majority of the peasantry. But whatever changes it made, it had to accept its profound moral obligation to mitigate the war's enormous material, social, and psychological damage to the people, and especially veterans; any economic strategy that failed to assign this responsibility the highest priority would inevitably alienate those who both expected and needed help most. The party could ill-afford to lose the people's confidence, and only its overweening arrogance of power and contempt for the masses has enabled it to do so. The wartime organizational system continued in various forms for another decade, and when it was abandoned virtually no attempt was made to preserve those rural cooperative institutions that retained great social and economic value and could have been the foundation of a reformed but essentially equitable land structure. Literally, a huge organizational void was created. The new land system is just as absolute and uncompromising as the old one, and it will soon harm the bulk of the peasants even more profoundly. In an agrarian nation, the party's handling of the land problem has unquestionably been its single greatest error.

As a significant portion of its members have become a decisive section of the ascendant economic elite, the Communists have increasingly divorced themselves from the masses. Urban labor is exploited ruthlessly, in conformity with the IMF's advice, to implement its fiscal conditions. When the Politburo embarked on the market line, its decisive constraints on debate necessarily created a total policy vacuum; by default, it ended by accepting essentially those programs the IMF, the World Bank, and its local followers advocated. Ironically, socialism's avowed enemies have had the decisive influence over its future. The East bloc nations and China did the same after 1986, with calamitous economic and political results. But the IMF and the World Bank's universal doctrinaire formula for ending poverty in the Third World has not been successful in the large majority of nations, and Vietnam is not likely to be an exception.

Instead, a dual economy and social system is emerging: a smaller part that is urbanized and unequal, but relatively much better off and growing, and the other largely very poor, predominantly rural, and with enduring social problems. If present trends continue, Vietnam's future crisis may in some crucial ways resemble those of the past: poor peasants and urban people excluded from the system's benefits will inevitably create a class basis for hostility to oppressive rulers, whether they call themselves Communists or anything else, and by means too diverse to predict may challenge them and undermine political stability. That an epic war should have been fought so that a class society might again be reestablished is a moral betrayal that defies description.

*

The Communists are taking great risks not simply because they are abandoning the masses who supported them in the past to economic and social insecurity, but especially because the general economic context for their gamble is essentially precarious. To succeed, all the elements involved must operate favorably, and they are not likely to do so because the progress Vietnam made after 1986 was largely the result of fortuitous but temporary circumstances rather than permanent structural changes. Most of it was unanticipated, reflecting ad hoc improvisations rather than a coherent strategy with reasonably predictable goals. The party expected large-scale foreign investment and the private sector to fuel economic growth, as if cheap labor would be sufficient to mobilize both, but neither materialized in the way or to the extent it anticipated. It was surprised when the state industries, which it had disparaged, more than filled the void and fueled most of the growth that had originally been anticipated from the private sector; but their managers have been compromising their very future by both legally and illegally confiscating an increasing portion of their assets. Its troop withdrawal from Cambodia had immense significance for Vietnam's position in the regional economy and the world economy, but it also made possible huge uncontrolled rice exports. By definition, these absolutely decisive stimuli cannot be repeated, and as their effects wear off the economy must slow down. Meanwhile, the nation's food supply is being gravely jeopardized. The Politburo encouraged foreign trade but soon lost control of smuggling, and Vietnam now has an increasingly onerous trade balance it is incapable of reversing; and it is falling more deeply into the classic Third World debt trap and dependency on foreign bankers.

Vietnam is no better able than Russia and China to create a true market economy from this eclectic porridge. Whatever emerges from this incongruous mixture of laissez faire and socialism is highly unlikely to be stable. Whatever the results, the party will try to retain control, but given its lack of coherence, it will be less and less able to do so. Its nominal mastery will be more symbolic than real. Whether it is formally replaced entirely or plays an increasingly ceremonial role that no longer shapes society is less certain than the fate of its original socialist goals. They will disappear.

For the first time since 1945, ordinary people with essentially economic grievances have begun to act openly against the party policies' material effects, and eventually they may pose a challenge to its control. As its market reforms produce mounting social instability in their wake, the party's declining legitimacy and authority will not allow it to avoid the inevitable consequences of a class structure based on inequality. Too many unresolved economic, social, and political problems exist in tandem, and as they increasingly intersect the party will not find solutions for them easily, if at all. An economic depression must affect socially marginalized poor people profoundly. In the end, the unpredictable but real ghosts of the class struggle may haunt those who continue to proclaim their belief in Marxism, producing both irony and tragedy. Should the party attempt to use the force at its command to cope with the masses' discontent, it will be trapped in a calamitous impasse of its own making. Will an army comprised of poor peasants repress other poor peasants? Can the party remain united under these circumstances?

It would be presumptuous of me to make exact predictions about what, much less when, people in Vietnam or any other country might do in the future. That actions seem logical under certain circumstances does not make them necessary, much less inevitable. Throughout history, the masses frequently fail to behave as we expect them to, but they also often become crucial catalysts of change when least anticipated. Suffice it to say that the internally divided and greatly weakened Communist party is confronting a growing array of complex tests involving the disenfranchised population. But even less-severe challenges have destroyed the parties of most other Communist states, and the ominous shadow their failures create for the party's leaders disturbs them profoundly – as indeed it should.

In its last stages, the most decisive and effective threat to all of the ruling Communist parties' hegemony has been from those leaders, apparatchiks, and technocrats within their own ranks whose consummate ambitions and absolute ideological neutrality caused them to transform the parties and their pretensions into personal political tools. Whenever they have acted, they have won! It is their very immunity from the masses that has enabled Communist leaders to abandon socialism and transform states into private rather than class property. Any party controlled by elites, whatever it calls itself, can easily betray its principles; where the masses have a real or potential role, their leaders' liberty is circumscribed. Whatever its faults, democracy within a party and nation is ultimately the only defense, if there is any at all, against moral treachery. Without a war, revolution, or any significant conflict, the international Communist movement has been virtually abolished, and never before in world history has such enormous power disappeared in such a docile, passive manner. This astonishing phenomenon was possible entirely because the people in absolute command of the parties were largely identical to those who gained the most from the new social systems that replaced the old. They remain in power, and the masses remain dispossessed.

The Buddhist opposition, Saigonese, and other dissidents whom the party attacks under the nebulous rubric of "peaceful evolution," are utterly insignificant compared to socialism's enemies within its own ranks and the state apparatus. The greatest immediate danger to the Vietnamese party is that it cannot trust a very significant portion of its own members. Its leaders will not or cannot constrain them, but the masses who are losing the most from their abuses and have most interest in controlling them have no way of doing so.

The Vietnamese people, especially the poor, saved the Communists from defeat during war, and today they alone have sufficient reasons to continue again with socialist economic principles and forms that are creatively adapted to reality and open to future modifications as needed. But the price of preventing Vietnam from becoming a hybrid variation of capitalism in fact, and socialist in name only, and of mobilizing the masses to reverse the trend, is democracy; the party's leaders will almost certainly prefer to continue as bourgeois authoritarians under the label of the Communist party than to risk genuine socialism with democracy. Their unyielding commitment to the dictatorship of the proletariat, which is tantamount to the party elite's power and growing privilege, will suffocate socialism fatally. Everywhere in the world, the logic of Communist authoritarianism has destroyed utterly its socialist ideals. If those within the party who still wish to save socialism do not once again rely upon the masses, Vietnam will also conform to this pattern.

Should this occur, the people will suffer the most, and their vast sacrifices be deceived.

Vo Nguyen Giap, the legendary architect of the Communists' military victory, recently explained how an army comprised of poor peasants had defeated the vastly larger and better-equipped French and American forces. "One must not confuse war with military decisions," he observed. "War is not a military strategy but a synthesis of the political, the military and the diplomatic. . . . Ultimately, war is a philosophy."[1]

The Communists never possessed a comparable philosophy of peace, and had they fought the war in the same improvised and confused fashion with which they have exploited its aftermath, they certainly would have lost it.

The entire historical experience, Vietnamese included, has repeatedly confirmed that a nation ultimately cannot truly win a war unless it is able also to utilize the period that follows it to attain the goals for which it struggled and sacrificed so much. By itself, holding power alone is not success, because it does not in the long run create the social legitimacy or mass support that is an absolute prerequisite for stability. In this crucial sense, the Communist party is in the process of losing its victory, and it is increasingly likely to suffer the same fate as all the other Communist nations: it will either disappear or, as in the case of China, linger on as a cynical mockery of the very concept of socialism.

The Vietnamese people earned and deserved far, far better. No one can ever fathom how much they suffered on behalf of their original ideals. If they lose the peace, their epic drama will become one more enormous tragedy, more ironic than most, in a century that has endured far greater misfortune than any in the history of civilization.

Epilogue
The necessity and risks of resisting injustice

The Vietnam War inspired what was by far this century's largest international protest movement on behalf of victims of oppression and violence. Whether this vast outpouring of solidarity made a significant difference to the Communists' final victory is far less crucial than its very existence: it was truly global, continued a relatively long time, and mobilized the passion, energy, and idealism of millions of people whose devotion created a world community that shared profound humanist values. Regardless of how Vietnam itself fares, which has always depended wholly on the Vietnamese themselves, the very emergence of such a massive antiwar movement will remain the war's enduring and positive legacy.

Those who opposed the war protested not just because of French and American intervention against Vietnam. The war was also an opportunity for countless people, horrified by the sustained, unconscionable conflicts that have blighted the entire century, finally to draw a symbolic line against the world's institutionalized violence and aggression. Socialists before 1914 had argued that international solidarity could prevent a terrible world conflagration, and their failure to act made possible the greatest tragedy of modern times, one that has since spawned unimaginable savagery and irrationality. The Spanish Civil War rekindled this internationalist ideal, but it was relatively brief and it never attained the anti-Vietnam War movement's intensity or vast scope. It justifiably inspired those who rightly have believed that internationalism's humanist and rational premises and goals are an essential even if not sufficient precondition for preventing or halting future barbarism. Because it was also a rejection of the violence and irrationality of our epoch, the unprecedented world antiwar movement's significance reached far beyond Vietnam itself.

The Vietnam War also evoked the passion of many of the Communist and Social Democratic parties' dissatisfied adherents, in addition to independent radicals, who by the early 1960s were chafing at the bureaucratic, cautious politics of the world's two principal socialist tendencies. In a century marred by cynicism and increasingly starved of idealism and noble causes, the antiwar movement involved countless people who were presented with an opportunity to express their latent social idealism, whether in demonstrations or innumerable other manifestations of their indignation. It dissolved many of the political constraints that the two exhausted socialist movements had imposed, and it contributed very significantly to the great European demonstrations in the spring of 1968, the fatal weakening of the European Communist parties, the emergence of the ecological and counterculture movements, and much else that has since changed political dialogue profoundly in many nations for the better. It was the harbinger of a critical consciousness that freed millions from the sclerosis that has inhibited leftist political dialogue since 1945. In the process, countless individuals made very great personal commitments and worked with astonishing devotion; many paid important personal prices that defined the remainder of their lives. In this important sense, as well, the antiwar movement transcended Vietnam itself; it was the beginning of a needed liberation from old shibboleths and a resurrection of neglected idealism. The antiwar movement, in essence, was a crucial transition between the staid 1950s, with its Cold War obsessions and paralyses, and the politics of the more unpredictable, critical period that has followed.

Nonetheless, while opposition to the sheer violence and destruction against a land and its people motivated all those who condemned the war, many of those who organized and led the movement assumed, if only implicitly, that something akin to a reasonably equitable society would emerge after the peace – if not entirely in fact, then at least in inspiration. While their principal objective was always to end the war, none could suspect that two decades after it ended Vietnam would adopt much of the culture and values that the United States had sought unsuccessfully to impose during the war. Given this paradox, everyone is obligated to ask who really won the war, and reflect profoundly on its true significance. If the Vietnamese people learn that their sacrifice was ultimately in vain, what then of those who solidarized with them?

Human choices everywhere, at all times, are limited by the constraints that historical circumstances impose upon them. If the ever-present risks of unanticipated tragic complications from our idealistic commitments and action were always to inhibit our resistance to social evils and war, people would constantly remain morally passive and tolerate injustice and oppression – with far greater dangers as a result.

Even if we wish to do so, or imagine that we can, so long as the world is so interdependent it is an illusion for anyone to suppose they can avoid the ultimate political and personal implications, both for themselves and for others, of injustice, war, and oppression. The question is not whether resistance to these indignities should occur but only how best to express it. Throughout this century, vast numbers of initially apolitical people believed that its terrible political convulsions would not also sweep them up, either as victims or resisters, but they ended as participants in the countless events, ranging from small meetings to revolutions, that produce great social changes. Few before momentous upheavals ever suspect the intensity of their own anger, or sense their capacity to act or its potential results.

The personal consequences of apathy in the face of evil must always be weighed against those of opposition to it, but there are serious risks either way. We can never avoid this dilemma so long as the world always imposes difficult choices upon us. Even if we weigh the moral and functional consequences of maintaining silence in the face of evil against support for a cause which then produces injustices of its own, this dilemma neither warrants, nor often allows, neutrality. The question is usually not whether to make a decision regarding our action but only when we will be obligated to do so, and whether it is best to do so earlier or later. But later, frequently, is often too late, the stakes greater and responses inherently more dangerous than if challenges had been confronted sooner. For most people, delays are far more common than timely action, and struggles are frequently fought after the possibilities of success have declined significantly. Postponement appears safer initially in many cases, but at the price of tolerating numerous injustices and remaining silent as they are occurring. To the extent it preempts and constrains those who may assault civilized society, idealism is also the logic of self-interest.

We can never know in advance the ultimate outcome of our actions in a world in which political forces and actors are inherently unstable, often in complex ways that they themselves fail to comprehend. If we were to ask for an absolute guarantee regarding the effects of our conduct, we would always remain passive, and the negative moral and functional results of our inertia would be far greater. Such assurances are neither desirable nor possible, and no one who relates to our world has ever had immunity from risks. Were we to demand certitude as the price of action, mankind's condition would be far worse than it is at present.

Even greater than the chance of making mistakes is stasis – paralysis – and the assumption that nothing can be learned or changed. But errors may be constructive if they are not fatal first and, above all, if we learn how to avoid them in the future. Commitment to a cause or position can never become an unconditional moral blank check. It must include an acute critical self-consciousness regarding the essential safeguards that protect intellectual, human, and political responses from illusions and abuses – and makes worthwhile a positive reaction to challenges we face. Ultimately, regardless of those who cause it, our safest guide is to oppose injustice and oppression wherever it exists and whenever we confront it. In a world full of ambiguous choices, this is our sole lifeline against sustained errors.

Profound social changes are invariably the result of cataclysms associated principally with wars and their aftermath, for they alone create the indispensable preconditions for vast transformations and then make it astonishingly easy for very small numbers of people to attain power. Had the Japanese not traumatized the Vietnamese people during World War Two it would have been impossible for several thousand young people, mainly students, in August 1945 to lead millions of peasants and take power. The Communist party no more made the revolution in Vietnam than it did in Russia in 1917 or China later. This pattern of Vietnamese socialism emerging out of the chaos of military conflicts became permanent when France and the United States spent three more decades assaulting the country, and they indelibly shaped and distorted Vietnam's institutions, including the present.

In this context, the Communist party's present grave predicament directly reflects its oppressors' legacies. It is the consummate irony – and tragedy – of this great epic that when the Communists began to search for economic alternatives to a war economy they chose those basic economic principles that the United States, far more than any other nation, has sought to impose upon the world. The International Monetary Fund and the World Bank in Washington only resumed where the Pentagon had failed. No one could conceivably have imagined that a titanic American military machine would be unable to impose its will after a decade of incredible destruction, much less that men in suits would easily do so over tables. The Vietnamese Communists, in the final analysis, were as weak after the war as they had been powerful during it, and now they are on the verge of disappearing in all but name.

All revolutions, ultimately, are created by old orders destroying themselves and creating vast social and ideological voids that others fill. In one fundamental sense, notwithstanding their sustained ineptness or irrelevance until the crucial moment, leaders are pushed to the fore by accident, when their luck is then transformed into grave responsibilities which require consummate wisdom and courage. The major tragedies of modern history are to a critical extent a part of an integral continuum, with cause and effect overlapping and merging and creating new forces that reflect, in often crucial ways, the influence of all that preceded them. This interaction is organizational, as older institutions and people survive in diverse forms, but it is also intellectual. It was its inability to transcend these lingering ideological legacies and influences that ultimately affected most of the world's Communist and socialist movements, and destroyed them. They did not merely fail to liberate themselves from the mental heritage of the old order: they never even acknowledged the problem, and in the end Adam Smith and David Ricardo have filled the huge analytic void always inherent in Marxism. We today live in an unimaginably complex and increasingly dangerous world attempting, both on the Left and the Right, to survive with the intellectual ghosts of the nineteenth century. The result is reflected in the massive ideological shambles at all points across the political spectrum.

In the last analysis, all successful Communist parties inherited bankrupt regimes that bequeathed them both their vast problems as well as immense opportunities. There is a tragic dialectic in decadent oppressive social orders that produce their own successors almost by chance, for the latter invariably fail. While the initial predicaments and constraints that revolutionaries in power confront are to a crucial extent imposed upon them, they have perpetuated them and failed to create more durable, just societies. In the present and former Communist states, the leaders and those they have anointed have merely become the new economic plutocrats, and class societies have now been formally established. But if oppressors defined indelibly the original parameters for those that replaced them, and to that extent share a very great measure of blame for everything that followed, it was never inevitable that those who succeeded them would accept their constraints. The absolutely essential freedom of imagination and analysis they required was axiomatically precluded in the case of the Communist parties. It was this, above all, that led to their ultimate failure.

Just as it was the legacies of Japanese, French, and American imperialisms that produced both the Vietnamese Communists' triumph and failure, it also made the emergence of an unprecedented world antiwar movement both possible and essential – and almost inevitable. Ultimately, all of the tragedies and ironies that the Vietnam experience created from 1945 until the present remain the responsibility of those who either began or favored the war, and they alone must accept the principal guilt for them all. Nothing that occurred in Vietnam throughout this century – or that happens in the future – can exonerate those who favored dominating and terrorizing many hapless poor countries with the whole range of American resources, ranging from organizing coup d'états to the massive bombing of civilians. If nations – of which the United States has been, by far, the foremost since 1945 – did not seek to rule over others then our century would have been spared unimaginable suffering and the monumental loss of lives and riches. It is against this great tragedy that countless men and women justifiably reacted, and whatever happened in Vietnam after 1975 in no way mitigates their noble motives and outrage. It would have been an unconscionable blot on mankind's moral consciousness had a vast antiwar movement not emerged to oppose the countless horrors the United States inflicted on Vietnam, just as it will always remain a crime against humanity that it embarked upon such a war. Nothing can ever change this fundamental moral equation, including the Communist leaders' later imposition of new injustices on their people. Indeed, it only makes all the more necessary our indignation over these rulers' betrayal of all those who suffered immeasurably and both earned and merited far, far better.

In a world full of continuous injustices, we never select the time and place we must confront them; those who create iniquities force choices upon us, and it will always remain that way. Because we live in human society as it is, whether we wish to or not we must function within those constraints inherent in this absence of freedom, and this necessarily constantly imposes difficult options upon us. History is never an open book that permits us to write out our desires and expect to achieve them. Profound ambiguities and dilemmas are always predictable, and for those who attempt to challenge mankind's evils there will always be enigmatic quandaries. Errors of judgment, either by omission or commission, are also inevitable. Good intentions can never wholly justify such mistakes but they are far less dangerous or morally culpable than apathy and egoism, which surrender by default to those who would perpetuate our world's follies and catastrophes.

If justice and rationality defined the major political experiences of our times then we would confront no great moral choices, and the inherent difficulty of the decisions we must make would have few consequences. We cannot escape politics and society, for they ignore no one, and it is an illusion to suppose we can somehow avoid their dangerous social consequences. Whether we are passive or active regarding them, our lives will be engulfed in major, sometimes critical, ways, and often such choices define the great challenges we all face during our lives and the kinds of human beings we will become. But even if we seek to make our world more rational and humane, there is no assurance whatsoever that we will change it sufficiently to reverse the tide of great events. The vast majority of idealists who attempt to do so fail, but there are also successes, at least in part. In a few rare but momentous occasions, some of these have a profound and decisive impact on the fate of nations and the people in them.

When people cease to be willing to accept these responsibilities when they should and must, a dark night of despair will overcome our world.

Notes

The *Daily Report* for East Asia, issued weekdays by the U.S.
Foreign Broadcast Information Service, is the principal source
for the entire Vietnamese press and radio. While it translates many
articles appearing in the more specialized official sources, it
routinely includes the texts of all key party documents and
leaders' statements. It is especially attentive to *Nhan Dan*, the
party's official daily newspaper, and *Tap Chi Cong San*, its theoretical monthly, the two most important publications. Unless otherwise indicated, all my quotations from party statements or by
members are taken from an authorized publication, but I also note
when they are specifically from these two sources, since they are
especially influential. A very small portion of the FBIS's output
comprises non-Vietnamese reports, and where I use them I
indicate their origin. In June 1996, I also used the FBIS East Asia
edition on the U.S. World News Connection (WNC edition),
Internet, which is different than the printed FBIS, and I have
indicated several of these citations in the notes by the FBIS code
appropriate for it. In 1996 I also received the full text of AP, AFP,
and Reuters wire dispatches on Vietnam, and they are indicated
simply as dispatches on file with those press services.

The following abbreviations are used in the footnotes:

BBC: *BBC Summary of World Broadcasts: Far East.* Issued weekdays
by BBC Monitoring. The date of issue and page number are noted.

FBIS: *Daily Report: East Asia,* of the U.S. Foreign Broadcast Information Service. The date of issue and page number are noted.

FER: *Far Eastern Economic Review.* Unless otherwise noted, all
articles until 1994 are by Murray Hiebert.

ILO: International Labour Organization, *Viet Nam: Labour and
Social Issues in a Transition Economy,* Bangkok, 1994.

IMF, 1994: International Monetary Fund, *Viet Nam* (IMF Economic Reviews, No. 13), Washington, DC, November 1994.

IMF, 1996: International Monetary Fund, *Vietnam: Transition to a Market Economy* (Occasional Paper 135), Washington, DC, March 1996.

ND: Nhan Dan. The Communist party's leading daily newspaper.

TC: Tap Chi Cong San. The Communist party's theoretical journal.

WB, 1993: The World Bank, East Asia and Pacific Region, *Viet Nam: Transition to the Market*, Washington, DC, September 1993.

WB, 1994: The World Bank, East Asia and Pacific Region, *Viet Nam: Poverty Assessment and Strategy*, Washington, DC, January 1995.

WB, 1995: The World Bank, East Asia and Pacific Region, *Viet Nam: Economic Report on Industrialization and Industrial Policy*, Washington, DC, October 17, 1995.

WB, 1996: The World Bank, *From Market to Plan: World Development Report 1996*, New York, Oxford University Press, 1996.

INTRODUCTION: THE LEGACY OF WAR

1   Tran Phuong stunned me in December 1973 when he said that after the war foreign investors would flock to Vietnam for its cheap labor! It was natural that he became a leading advocate of the market line, which he justified in Marxist terms as both inevitable and desirable. His unique ability to evoke Marxist doctrine to justify the Politburo's line, whatever it was, was the key to his remarkable rise to authority. He was responsible for many of the major economic errors in the early 1980s, which the Politburo later blamed on dogmatism.

2   The historical disproof of the market's role in economic development is overwhelming. For the market internationally, see especially Bairoch (1989; 1993). For its irrelevance to domestic economic experiences, see Kolko (1963).

CHAPTER 1: THE POSTWAR ECONOMY AND THE ORIGINS OF "MARKET SOCIALISM"

1   Nayan Chanda in *FER*, January 9, 1981, p. 40.

2   Vo Nhan Tri, in Nguyen Duc Nhuan (1987, pp. 50–8); William S. Turley, in Turley and Selden (1993, pp. 23–4).

3   Le Duan, December 8, 1983, in *Vietnam Courier* (Hanoi), February 1984, p. 2.

4 Stern (1985, p. 533). See also *New York Times*, August 9, 1964; August 30, 1964; Senator Gravel Edition, *The Pentagon Papers*, Boston, Mass., Beacon Press, 1971, vol. 2, p. 353.
5 Stern, op. cit., p. 532.
6 See ibid., pp. 530–6 for the Chinese resurgence. Also see Turley, op. cit., pp. 24, 202; *Christian Science Monitor*, August 12, 1982; IMF, "Viet Nam Staff report for the 1983 Article IV Consultation," SM/83/123, June 13, 1983, p. 12; Tri, op. cit., p. 148. Since the IMF was providing small credits in this period, it gave advice in 1981 on prices and exchange rates, which was largely accepted. Even if in minor ways, it was always on the scene.
7 *ND*, in *BBC*, March 4, 1986, p. K/1.
8 See the references in my Introduction, note 2.

CHAPTER 2: ECONOMIC REFORM IN THEORY AND PRACTICE

1 *BBC*, March 4, 1986, p. K/1.
2 IMF, 1996, p. 28.
3 *FER*, October 1, 1987, p. 95; January 14, 1988, pp. 48–9; Asian Development Bank, *Asian Development Outlook 1989*, Manila, 1989, pp. 98–101; IMF, 1994, p. 57; FBIS, June 22, 1988, p. 45; *ND*, FBIS, July 15, 1988, p. 55.
4 *International Herald Tribune*, July 13, 1982; IMF, "Staff Report . . .", SM/82/84 (April 30, 1982); SM/83/123 (June 13, 1983).
5 Nayan Chanda, *FER*, October 1, 1987, p. 70.
6 World Bank, "Fact Sheet: Vietnam and the World Bank – Partners in Progress," [ca. June 1996], p. 1. The Bank played a crucial and growing role notwithstanding that it was not until November 1993 that it actually began lending to Vietnam. The Politburo's expectations were sufficient to guide its policies, revealing that it was extremely vulnerable to baits – which cost the Bank nothing in the short run.
7 IMF, 1994, p. 1. See also IMF, *Annual Report, 1994*, Washington, DC, 1994, p. 116.
8 *Transition* (World Bank), November–December 1995, p. 5.
9 *IMF Survey*, July 1, 1996, p. 213.
10 Ibid., pp. 214, 216.
11 Quoted in William S.Turley, in Turley and Selden (1993, p. 9).
12 FBIS, April 28, 1989, p. 85.
13 Ibid., p. 86.
14 *The Financial Times*, June 9, 1989.
15 Sixth plenum resolution, FBIS, April 28, 1989, p. 87.
16 FBIS, April 16, 1996, p. 89.
17 FBIS, January 24, 1994, p. 70.
18 FBIS, April 1, 1994, p. 58.

19   *TC*, FBIS, September 12, 1989, pp. 65–6; typescript text of Thach speech to seventh party congress, June 25, 1991, p. 3.
20   *BBC*, July 5, 1991, C 1/1.
21   FBIS, July 2, 1993, p. 42; February 28, 1994, p. 71.
22   FBIS, February 19, 1991, pp. 55–6.
23   Phan Van Khai, in FBIS, December 1, 1994, p. 47.
24   FBIS, January 24, 1994, p. 68.
25   FBIS, March 25, 1994, p. 53.
26   FBIS, May 29, 1991, p. 40; draft platform, FBIS, December 5, 1990, p. 64.
27   *ND*, FBIS, April 1, 1994, p. 59.
28   WB, 1995, p. 25, table 2.2B; WB, 1993, p. 235; IMF, 1996, pp. 6, 11, 13, 46–7; *IMF Survey*, March 19, 1996, p. 99.
29   WB, 1995, p. 25; "A Survey of Business in Asia," *The Economist*, March 9, 1996, p. 10; East Asia Analytic Unit, Department of Foreign Affairs and Trade [Australia], *Overseas Chinese Business Networks in Asia*, Canberra, 1995, pp. 85, 149.
30   IMF, 1996, p. 9.
31   *IMF Survey*, March 19, 1996, p. 99; IMF, 1996, pp. 24, 53; WB, 1995, p. 4, table 6.1A; WB, 1993, p. 248; FBIS, June 27, 1995, p. 70; *Asia Times*, January 3, 1996; *International Herald Tribune*, January 17, 1996.
32   WB, 1993, p. 240; WB, 1995, table 3.2; IMF, 1994, p. 61; ILO, pp. 6–9; *IMF Survey*, July 26, 1993, p. 240; IMF, 1996, p. 33. I was in frequent contact with Vietnamese oil personnel, up to the highest level, from 1971 to about 1977, and under the crucial direction of Dr Michael Tanzer, an outstanding independent oil consultant who met with them extensively both in Hanoi and Paris and also provided essential background, helped introduce them to basic problems and sources of information. The oil sector's literacy and skill was unique, and it was no accident that it later became so important. Had comparable efforts been undertaken in other fields before 1975, Vietnam's economy would have been far more successful. The official ideology had nothing whatsoever to do with oil's performance, and had it not been run by able people it would have failed regardless of doctrine. It merely revealed that information is a precondition of any policy, and without it they will all fail.
33   IMF, 1996, p. 48; WB, 1996, p. 220; *The Financial Times*, November 25, 1995; December 15, 1995; May 21, 1996; July 30, 1996; *International Herald Tribune*, January 17, 1996; WB, 1995, table 3.1; FBIS, June 4, 1996, p. 70. The 1995 official current account deficit was 8 percent of the GDP, but 15 percent if smuggling is included. Even 8 percent is very high. See Adam Schwarz, *FER*, April 25, 1996; AFP dispatch, Hanoi, December 4, 1996.
34   *The Financial Times*, August 19, 1996. A World Bank report in late 1996 described the state banking system as technically bankrupt by international standards. AFP dispatch, Hanoi, November 13, 1996.
35   IMF, 1996, p. 51.
36   FBIS, March 14, 1995, p. 69.
37   *The Financial Times*, October 17, 1995. Fiscal decentralization restricts

essential larger infrastructure projects and thereby retards growth; see Tao Zhang and Heng-fu Zou (1996).

38 *The Financial Times*, November 3, 21, and 25, 1995; January 3, 1996; June 27, 1996; AFP dispatch, Hanoi, July 29, 1996; IMF, 1996, p. 17; FBIS, March 24, 1995, p. 58; February 21, 1996, p. 93. By 1996 the state bank implicitly acknowledged that only more domestic funds would enable it to meet the target. *TC*, FBIS, May 22, 1996, p. 90.

39 *Transition* (World Bank), November–December 1995, p. 5. See also IMF, 1996, p. 16.

40 WB, 1993, pp. 33–4, 39, 83–5, 223–9; Jonathan Moore, *FER*, August 30, 1990; *The Financial Times*, February 24, 1994; *Vietnam Economic Times*, June 1994, pp. 8–11; Hiebert (1996, p. 143).

41 Many Chinese who favor outright privatization admit that the only way to attain it is informally. As a World Bank expert states it: "Because of political constraints ... another view, shared by those who support privatization, spontaneous privatization and insider control by managers and workers is the (second) best choice for China, because formal privatization is impossible. The needed strategy [is] ... to continue the trend of giving the managers more control and eventually making them *de facto* owners" (Yingyi Qian, 1995, p. 238).

42 WB, 1995, p. 103.

43 WB, 1993, p. 48.

44 WB, 1995, pp. 25, 32, 97.

45 Ibid., p. 103.

46 Ibid., pp. 8–11, table 2.1B, table 5.2B; IMF, 1996, p. 51; FBIS, March 17, 1995, p. 79.

47 Quoted in Porter (1993, p. 147). See also ibid., pp. 130–3; Probert and Young (1995, pp. 507–9). See *ND*, FBIS, January 5, 1988, pp. 50–2 for the new policy on SOEs.

48 WB, 1993, p. 44; WB, 1995, pp. 26, 112, 117; IMF, 1996, pp. 14–15; AFP dispatch, Hanoi, August 1,1996; *ND*, FBIS, January 5, 1988, pp. 50–2.

49 WB, 1993, p. 44.

50 WB, 1996, p. 50.

51 *TC*, FBIS, May 22, 1996, pp. 99–100.

52 FBIS, July 20, 1995, p. 102.

53 WB, 1995, p. 26.

54 Probert and Young (1995, pp. 513–16).

55 FBIS, December 7, 1993, p. 73.

56 WB, 1993, p. 20.

57 FBIS, February 15, 1994, p. 65.

58 FBIS, January 24, 1994, p. 70.

59 WB, 1996, p. 50.

60 IMF, 1994, p. 8; *TC*, FBIS, October 3, 1995, p. 98; April 16, 1996, p. 88; May 21, 1996, p. 102; WB, 1995, p. 99.

61 WB, 1995, pp. 105–6; WB, 1993, p. 53; FBIS, June 8, 1995, p. 69; FBIS, August 3, 1995, p. 83. Workers also oppose formal privatization since a large part of SOE profits, such as are left, go to them in welfare payments. Probert and Young (1995, pp. 501, 517).

62 IMF, 1994, p. 9. See also WB, 1995, p. 109.

63 *TC*, FBIS, October 3, 1995, p. 101.

64 Ibid.

65 Ministry officials personally bought 40 percent and kept 18 percent in their ministry's control, giving them absolute power. See Hiebert (1996, p. 69).

CHAPTER 3: THE COMMUNIST PARTY'S POLITICAL CRISIS

1 *TC*, FBIS, March 25, 1994, p. 51.

2 Carlyle A. Thayer, "Mono-organizational Socialism and the State," in Benedict J. Tria Kerkvliet and Doug J. Porter (eds), *Vietnam's Rural Transformation*, Boulder, Col., Westview Press, 1995, pp. 47, 55–6.

3 See the political report, central committee, FBIS, February 15, 1994, p. 71, on "revolutionary morality."

4 Vo Dai in *World Economic Problems* (Hanoi), December 1988, p. 22; Do Muoi in FBIS, July 9, 1990, p. 55.

5 Do Muoi, FBIS, December 7, 1993, p. 75; FBIS, December 7, 1990, p. 57.

6 FBIS, February 15, 1994, p. 68; *ND*, FBIS, April 1, 1994, p. 58.

7 *ND*, FBIS, April 1, 1994, p. 58.

8 Do Muoi, FBIS, January 25, 1994, p. 69.

9 FBIS, June 27, 1995, p. 69; October 5, 1995, p. 84.

10 Porter (1993, pp.101–3, 114–17, 121–7); *FER*, June 13, 1991.

11 FBIS, June 6, 1995, p. 86.

12 Porter (1993, p. 71). By 1994, over 50 percent of the party's members had joined after 1975; FBIS, August 10, 1994, p. 98.

13 *BBC*, August 22, 1986, p. K/6; *Vietnam Courier*, December 1987, p. 4.

14 *ND*, FBIS, April 8, 1991, p. 70. In 1994, somewhat less than half the party's cadres lived in rural areas, which contained about 80 percent of the population. *TC*, FBIS, March 25, 1994, p. 45.

15 Do Muoi, FBIS, August 26, 1991, p. 67. A 1988 survey of a large sample of rural members concluded that 16 percent seriously violated party rules on corruption and discipline; that share is much higher today. See Porter (1993, p. 71).

16 David W. P. Elliott, in Turley and Selden (1993, p. 84).

17 FBIS, March 1, 1995, p. 84.

18 FBIS, July 11, 1996, p. 95.

19 FBIS, April 12, 1996, p. 98.

20 *ND*, FBIS, June 3, 1996, p. 95.

21 Do Muoi, FBIS, February 15, 1994, p. 61; *TC*, FBIS, March 25, 1994, p. 46.

22 FBIS, February 6, 1995, p. 99.

23 FBIS, April 7, 1995, p. 71.

24 FBIS, February 22, 1996, pp. 87–9; March 1, 1996, pp. 71–2; March 6, 1996, p. 82; July 11, 1996, p. 95; Reuters dispatch, January 30, 1996.

25 WB, 1993, p. vii; Turley and Selden (1993, p. 84). Ironically, the IMF's own experts acknowledge that the low wages they advocate must lead to, and thereby implicitly justify, corruption. See Vito Tanzi, "Cor-

ruption, Governmental Activities, and Markets," *Finance and Development*, December 1995, pp. 24–6.

26 ILO, p. 11; WB, 1993, p. vii; FBIS, October 23, 1995, p. 85; March 29, 1996, p. 63.

27 FBIS, October 23, 1995, p. 85; July 20, 1995, p. 103.

28 FBIS, July 20, 1995, p. 102.

29 Le Duc Anh confirms that the party operates business enterprises. See FBIS, July 10, 1996, p. 98. *The Financial Times*, July 19, 1996, revealed that the central committee had in 1995 created a unit, Truong An, that was negotiating participation in a $250 million fund that would invest in capital-intensive projects. It is less important that this deal is reached than the very fact the party is prepared to enter into it. See also *The Financial Times*, August 21, 1996.

30 FBIS, June 2, 1993, p. 57.

31 FBIS, August 3, 1994, p. 73.

32 See *FER*, July 30, 1992; February 10, 1994; Do Muoi, FBIS, January 24, 1994, p. 67; Do Muoi, FBIS, February 15, 1994, pp. 61, 72; *International Herald Tribune*, April 11, 1996. Corruption in 1993 was far higher than in 1992 – by a factor of perhaps three or four. See *TC*, FBIS, May 26, 1994, p. 54. The 1996 party congress political report asserts that "a portion" of the members are rotten, leaving the magnitude of the problem open. FBIS, April 17, 1996, p. 93.

33 FBIS, August 15, 1990, p. 69.

34 *The Financial Times*, February 8, 1996; *Indochina Chronology*, October–December 1995, p. 7; Robert Templer, AFP dispatch, Hanoi, June 16, 1996; Probert and Young (1995, p. 522).

35 *ND*, FBIS, November 1, 1994, p. 74.

36 Ibid.

37 *ND*, FBIS, October 3, 1995, p. 92.

38 FBIS, November 23, 1994, p. 69. The government since 1993 has privatized urban housing, selling it to those tenants willing to buy their homes. Officials living in the best housing thereby bought villas at bargain prices, and many have resold or are renting them for large windfalls. Housing speculation is rife and illegal land deals widespread – and tolerated. See "Vietnam: New Land Laws," International Trade Administration, U.S. Department of Commerce (IMI960909), September 11, 1996.

39 FBIS, March 29, 1995, p. 73; April 7, 1995, p. 72; July 12, 1995, p. 103; July 21, 1995, p. 67; March 20, 1996, pp. 88–9.

40 *TC*, FBIS, January 29, 1996, pp. 65–7; March 29, 1996, p. 64.

41 FBIS, July 2, 1994, p. 100. In 1995, only a small minority of violators was accused, and of these only one in twenty were charged – and fewer yet condemned. FBIS, March 6, 1996, p. 82.

42 *TC*, FBIS, July 21, 1995, p. 67.

43 FBIS, June 12, 1992, p. 40.

44 FBIS, March 4, 1994, p. 71.

45 FBIS, October 23, 1995, p. 85.

46 Le Phuoc Tho, FBIS, February 22, 1996, p. 90; *TC*, FBIS, May 26, 1994, p. 52.

47 FBIS, December 5, 1990, p. 62.

48 FBIS, May 12, 1989, p. 57.
49 FBIS, December 5, 1990, p. 69.
50 *BBC*, February 13, 1990, B/4.
51 See, esp., *ND*, FBIS, October 3, 1991, p. 58. The June 1989 events in China and the collapse of the Soviet bloc compelled the party to reconsider the sources of the global Communist crisis, and while it acknowledged the "mistakes in socialist construction in the Soviet Union," the events there ultimately caused it to abandon many of the verbal concessions it had made to the increased freedom of ideas. FBIS, June 14, 1991, p. 35; September 13, 1991, p. 80. Hanoi initially remained neutral on China's turmoil, but it unequivocally attacked the opposition in Poland and Hungary, and eventually discreetly endorsed Peking's repressive policies. See *BBC*, June 9, 1989, A3/2; FBIS, August 18, 1989, p. 52; August 28, 1989, pp. 54–5.
52 FBIS, September 29, 1995, p. 95.
53 *TC*, FBIS, April 17, 1996, p. 97.
54 *TC*, FBIS, January 29, 1996, p. 67.
55 FBIS, May 31, 1996, p. 94.
56 FBIS, April 16, 1996, p. 96.
57 Ibid.

CHAPTER 4: LAND AND THE CRISIS OF RURAL SOCIETY

1 The redistribution of land has proceeded very unequally: quickly in the southern Mekong Delta but much more slowly in the Red River Delta, where population density makes cooperative systems highly rational for the peasants. Every step in this transformation involves major stakes for them. If the peasants had been asked to vote, they probably would have rejected both the prereform land system and the alternative imposed upon them.
2 *ND*, FBIS, May 27, 1996, FBIS-EAS-96-110 (WNC edition), pp. 3, 6, 9.
3 *TC*, FBIS, June 15, 1994, p. 72.
4 FBIS, July 20, 1988, p. 39.
5 *TC*, FBIS, June 15, 1994, p. 71. See also Benedict J. Tria Kerkvliet, in Kerkvliet and Porter (1995, p. 74). My national estimate adjusts for those regions in the south where coops never existed.
6 *TC*, FBIS, December 1, 1994, p. 52; *TC*, FBIS, May 26, 1994, p. 54.
7 *TC*, FBIS, July 21, 1995, p. 68. In May 1996 about 400 peasants who were being forced off their land so that a golf course could be built fought a pitched battle with police, injuring several dozen of them. One woman was killed. FBIS, May 21, 1996, p. 100.
8 Tran Thi Van Anh and Nguyen Manh Huan, in Kerkvliet and Porter (1995, p. 213).
9 FBIS, March 15, 1996, p. 73.
10 FBIS, June 15, 1994, p. 71.

11 *TC*, FBIS, March 25, 1994, p. 46.
12 *TC*, FBIS, July 21, 1995, p. 67.
13 *TC*, FBIS, July 22, 1994, p. 59.
14 ILO, pp. 14–19; Nguyen Van Thanh and Tran Thi Tuyet Mai, in *Vietnam's Socio-economic Development* (Hanoi), Summer 1995, p. 43; *Vietnamese Trade Unions* (Hanoi), No. 4, 1995, p. 27; FBIS, April 10, 1996, p. 72; April 12, 1996, p. 103.
15 *TC*, FBIS, July 22, 1994, p. 71. See also Thanh and Mai, op. cit., p. 47; *TC*, FBIS, April 12, 1996, pp. 102–3; Tran Lan Huong, "The Effect of Democratisation on the Transition to a Market Economy in the Countryside," pp. 3–5 (a longer version of an article in *TC*, April 1994, pp. 45–8, in my possession).
16 Hiebert (1996, p. 96) describes a working family of four earning the equivalent of $4.50 a month – and is starving!
17 WB, 1993, p. 207.
18 Quoted in Ngo Vinh Long, in Turley and Selden (1993, p. 192). The goal of a class structure is explicitly acknowledged in *TC*, FBIS, July 22, 1994, pp. 64, 71–3.
19 WB, 1994, p. 75.
20 FBIS, July 28, 1993, p. 87; *FER*, January 13, 1994, p. 71; WB, 1994, p. 13. A more recent survey in *TC*, FBIS, April 12, 1996, pp. 102–5, shows the situation has not improved since then, and may have worsened. In general, "40–50 percent of the production households do not have enough to eat. . . ." Ibid., p. 103.
21 FBIS, June 16, 1993, p. 52.
22 FBIS, July 11, 1996, p. 91.
23 *IMF Survey*, July 1, 1996, p. 215.
24 Quoted in Kerkvliet and Porter (1995, p. 73).

CHAPTER 5: THE SOCIAL AND HUMAN COSTS OF REFORM

1 *ND*, FBIS, March 1, 1996, p. 72; *TC*, FBIS, March 15, 1996, p. 73.
2 *Vietnam's Socio-economic Development*, Summer 1995, p. 73.
3 Do Muoi, FBIS, June 14, 1993, p. 68; Keith Richburg in *Washington Post* National Weekly edn, May 21–7, 1990; FBIS, August 18, 1993, p. 43; *FER*, January 13, 1994; 5th plenum resolution, FBIS, July 2, 1993, p. 42; *TC*, July 1995, in *Eglises d'Asie* (Paris), No. 210, December 1995, p. 8; *Vietnam's Socio-economic Development*, Summer 1995, p. 73.
4 WB, 1996, pp. 196–7; Asian Development Bank, *Asian Development Outlook 1990*, Manila, 1990, p. 119; WB, 1993, pp. 199–205; FBIS, November 7, 1994, p. 89; IMF, 1996, p. 51. Measures to introduce a progressive tax were initiated only in mid-1996. Whether they will be effective is another question. *The Financial Times*, July 27–8, 1996.
5 WB, 1994, pp. 2, 7.
6 Ibid., pp. 3, 12–15; WB, 1993, p. 249; ILO, 12.

7   *ND*, FBIS, March 20, 1996, p. 95. See also WB, 1995, table 7.1; FBIS, March 9, 1995, p. 48; October 3, 1995, p. 92.

8   ILO, p. 1; WB, 1993, pp. 134, 240, 248; FBIS, March 9, 1995, p. 47; Hiebert (1996, p. 86); IMF, 1996, p. 24.

9   FBIS, September 14, 1995, p. 53. Restrictions on rice exports will be phased out after 1996, further reducing the domestic supply. AP dispatch, Hanoi, December 3, 1996.

10 *ND*, FBIS, March 20, 1996, p. 96. See also WB, 1995, table 7.1. In the summer of 1996 the chairman of Vietnam's population control organization stated that population growth since 1930 had entirely offset the increase in rice output, and per capita availability in 1990 had not increased since then. AFP dispatch, September 5, 1996.

11 WB, 1993, pp. 240, 248; WB, 1995, table 7.1. This average does not describe what the majority of the population actually eats, for the upper fifth consumes about twice as many calories as the lowest. There are various criteria for human food requirements, and 365 kilos is only one that is often used. The UN Food and Agriculture Organization has its own, which is even more critical of Vietnam's performance. In 1990–2, the latest available data, Vietnam had a per capita availability of only 77 percent of its global kilocalorie requirements, of which rice was only one essential source. FAO (Bangkok office), private communication, May 1, 1996. Vietnam was, and remains, food poor.

12 *IMF Survey*, July 1, 1996, pp. 214–15.

13 WB, 1993, pp. 159, 22.

14 WB, 1996, p. 130.

15 Henry Kamm, *New York Times*, June 4, 1992 and May 6, 1993; *FER*, December 2, 1993; FBIS, March 29, 1995, p. 72; WB, 1996, p. 198.

16 FBIS, March 6, 1996, p. 80; *TC*, FBIS, June 4, 1996, p. 84.

17 *FER*, February 4, 1993.

18 WB, 1993, pp. 187ff; WB, 1994, p. 82; FBIS, March 29, 1995, p. 70; Hiebert (1996, pp. 184–6).

19 WB, 1993, p. 187.

20 FBIS, October 20, 1995, p. 57.

21 *Vietnamese Trade Unions* (Hanoi), No. 4, 1995, p. 28.

22 Chanda, in *FER*, September 7, 1989; FBIS, August 29, 1990, p. 58; *FER*, April 4, 1991; February 4, 1993; May 27, 1993, p. 60; September 2, 1993; Ian Simpson in *The Financial Times*, December 20, 1993; FBIS, December 18, 1990, p. 53; March 8, 1991, p. 67. In May 1994, Politburo member Vu Oanh described "about half" of the rural work force as "unemployed." FBIS, May 19, 1994, p. 72. The risk of the general rural situation leading to "social explosions" is acknowledged in *TC*, FBIS, May 26, 1994, p. 54. Popular discontent on unemployment is revealed in FBIS, June 15, 1994, p. 62. In May 1996 even city officials admitted that the actual unemployed in Hanoi were nearly twice the number registered. See *Vietnam Investment Review* in FBIS-EAS-96-108 (WNC edition); ILO, pp. vi, 13, 18. In November 1996 Western experts estimated Vietnam's general unemployment was about 20 percent, the highest in Asia. AFP dispatch, Hanoi, November 29, 1996.

23 *IMF Survey*, July 1, 1996, p. 214.

24 This index does not measure social security, health, and education expenses, which would cause real income to decline even further. FBIS, April 10, 1996, p. 73. See also ILO, p. 11; *FER*, January 25, 1996, p. 21.

25 *IMF Survey*, July 1, 1996, p. 216.

26 FBIS, September 26, 1995, p. 93.

27 FBIS, September 26, 1995, p. 93; May 8, 1996, p. 64; *FER*, January 25, 1996, p. 21; IMF, 1994, p. 10; *Asian Labour Update* (Hong Kong), August–October 1995, pp. 25–7.

28 By March 1996, senior officials admitted that the minimum wage was now meaningless, but that it had to be kept the lowest by regional standards. FBIS, April 10, 1996, p. 73.

29 FBIS, August 5, 1994, p. 84.

30 FBIS, March 11, 1996, p. 97.

31 Quoted in Greenfield (1997, p. 211).

32 FBIS, June 30, 1989, p. 59; *FER*, September 7, 1989; FBIS, June 2, 1993, p. 55.

33 FBIS, February 9, 1993, p. 70.

34 *FER*, September 2, 1993; Bruce Stanley, AP dispatch, Hanoi, May 26, 1994. Over seventy strikes occurred in the four years ending July 1994, according to FBIS, August 9, 1994, p. 95.

35 FBIS, February 15, 1994, p. 68.

36 FBIS, June 20, 1994, p. 73. See also ibid., pp. 71–3, where "hot discussions," "differing views," and the like are officially admitted; FBIS, February 23, 1994, p. 42; June 17, 1994, pp. 56–7; *Vietnam Economic Times*, June 1994, p. 4, on official unions' criticisms. That the labor law would work against strikes and workers' rights has since been verified in FBIS, August 5, 1994, pp. 95–7; August 9, 1994, pp. 89–92; August 22, 1994, p. 87; August 29, 1994, p. 88.

37 FBIS, September 26, 1995, p. 93.

38 FBIS, April 24, 1996, p. 84.

39 FBIS, April 2, 1996, p. 94.

40 FBIS, August 9, 1994, p. 97.

41 *FER*, January 25, 1996, p. 22; FBIS, April 25, 1996, p. 72.

CHAPTER 6: WHO RULES, AND WHY?

1 *The Financial Times*, August 6, 1996.

2 IMF, 1996, p. 1.

3 FBIS, June 27, 1995, p. 69.

4 ILO, pp. 34–5; WB, 1994, pp. viii, 13–15, 89–90, 112, 211; FBIS, January 6, 1995, p. 82.

5 *TC*, July 1995, reprinted in *Eglises d'Asie*, December 1995, p. 4. The 1996 party congress political report acknowledged that nepotism is a serious problem and must be dealt with; FBIS, April 17, 1996, p. 94.

6 *TC*, FBIS, July 22, 1994, p. 64.

7 FBIS, July 2, 1996, p. 85. Even in the late 1980s, while party members themselves were banned from doing so, the families of half the party

members in Ho Chi Minh City and 14 percent in Hanoi were engaged in capitalist activities. See Porter (1993, pp. 70–1).

8   FBIS, July 1, 1996, p. 55.

9   *FER*, February 29, 1996, pp. 42–4.

10 6th plenum resolution, FBIS, May 3, 1989, p. 78.

11 FBIS, January 22, 1990, p. 56.

12 FBIS, February 8, 1991, p. 73.

13 Bui Tin (1995). In December 1987, when I met Bui Tin in Hanoi, he spent an hour inundating me with photos of his past exploits.

14 FBIS, September 19, 1989, p. 60; December 14, 1989, p. 58.

15 FBIS, September 8, 1992, p. 40. See also *Vietnam Courier*, November 1984, p. 20; *FER*, March 5, 1987; FBIS, January 8, 1990, p. 69.

16 FBIS, September 15, 1992, p. 45.

17 FBIS, July 20, 1994, pp. 68–9.

18 FBIS, February 24, 1995, p. 78.

19 *TC*, FBIS, January 25, 1996, p. 83.

20 FBIS, November 3, 1994, p. 66.

21 FBIS, July 30, 1996, p. 98. Later, three important party officials were arrested for releasing Kiet's allegedly top-secret appeal to the Politburo, and in August 1996 two were sentenced to prison. They almost certainly did so in an effort to hinder it. See also *FER*, March 7, 1996, pp. 14–15; *The Financial Times*, August 23, 1996; AFP dispatch, Hanoi, August 22, 1996.

22 World Bank, Fact Sheet: "Vietnam and the World Bank – Partners in Progress," [ca. June 1996], p. 2. Vietnam was unable to tap the IMF's general resources until this time also. The size of the IMF and Bank staff includes consultants, who comprise the larger part; hence it varies. Conversation with Mr Thang Long Ton, Vietnam country team, World Bank, Washington, DC, October 7, 1996.

23 Dana Orange, External Affairs, East Asia and Pacific Region, World Bank, to author, August 23, 1996.

24 IMF conditions range from general to specific criteria, depending on its political priorities and objectives. The public sector's size and role is a key factor, and the IMF often insists on its reduction before releasing funds. It monitors performance criteria, if necessary, on a monthly basis. Its "conditionality" is potentially decisive to a weak nation's basic economic policy. See *IMF Survey*, September 1996, pp. 10–11.

25 Dana Orange, External Affairs, East Asia and Pacific Region, World Bank, to author, August 23, 1996.

26 *Bangkok Post* in FBIS, November 1, 1995, p. 74. The outline of the plan is in FBIS, November 14, 1995, p. 87; see also *New York Times*, October 29, 1995. This new arrangement concentrates far greater power in the prime minister's hands. The National Assembly passes laws but they are wholly contingent on the prime minister's implementing decrees, which provide decisive substantive form to them. See "Vietnam: New Land Laws," International Trade Administration, U.S. Department of Commerce (IMI960909), September 11, 1996.

27 FBIS, January 29, 1996, p. 64.

28 A very knowledgeable journalist who was at this November 27, 1995 meeting at the School of Oriental and Asian Studies with Callisto Madavo, then head of the Vietnam department, took detailed notes and gave them to me. Quotes are taken from them. See also *The Financial Times*, October 11, 1995; FBIS, November 21, 1995, p. 76.

29 World Bank release No. 96/4 EAP, December 1, 1995; FBIS, December 4, 1995, p. 70.

30 Ibid.

31 *IMF Survey*, March 19, 1996, p. 99.

32 *The Financial Times*, May 10, 1996. See also World Bank press release, Hanoi, May 9, 1996; *The Financial Times*, September 27, 1996.

33 FBIS, May 15, 1996, p. 89.

34 *The Financial Times*, May 21, 1996. The final details of this package were still unresolved in November 1996. The creditors' offer was less generous than their promise. See *The Financial Times*, November 19, 1996.

35 FBIS, July 11, 1996, p. 79; *ND*, FBIS, April 9, 1996, p. 97.

36 *FER*, July 11, 1996, p. 16. See also *Wall Street Journal*, June 28, 1996. In early December 1996, the donor nations and organizations convened their annual meeting in Hanoi. They rarely meet in the developing countries receiving aid, and this gesture was perceived rightfully as blatant direct intervention and further aid to Kiet's alliance. Given Vietnam's critical trade deficit and growing vulnerability, the donors offered unprecedentedly blunt advice on its need to conform even more quickly and strictly to IMF standards. The state industries were especially condemned. If Vietnam cooperated fully, an additional $2.4 billion in loans and grants was pledged – making the whole un-disbursed aid package about $9 billion. As a World Bank spokesman put it frankly, "We are saying if you want billions in foreign investment and aid then you have to accelerate the movement forward." AFP dispatch, Hanoi, December 4, 1996. Kiet's alliance and the World Bank-led coalition simply ignored the party's June 1996 decisions, another reflection on its growing irrelevance, and used their financial leverage without stint. In effect, they are seeking to buy Vietnam's future. "[T]he tougher part of the journey is still ahead," Phan Van Khai warned. *Asia Times*, December 6, 1996. See also *The Financial Times*, December 4 1996; *International Herald Tribune*, December 7–8, 1996; *Asia Times*, December 9, 1996.

37 *FER*, March 7, 1996, p. 15.

38 FBIS, March 20, 1996, p. 80.

39 FBIS, February 2, 1996, p. 66.

40 FBIS, May 31, 1996, p. 97; see also Reuters dispatch, Hanoi, June 10, 1996.

41 FBIS, June 13, 1996, pp. 85–7.

42 FBIS, June 21, 1996, p. 72.

43 FBIS, June 27, 1996, pp. 41–3.

44 *TC*, FBIS, August 17, 1995, p. 69.

45 *TC*, FBIS, January 29, 1996, pp. 65–7; *Asian Wall Street Journal*, June 28, 1996.

46 FBIS, October 20, 1995, p. 57.
47 IMF, 1996, p. 1.
48 The original statute is in FBIS, January 24, 1996, pp. 102–5.
49 FBIS, July 10, 1996, pp. 97–9; August 7, 1996, pp. 64–7.

CONCLUSION

1 *Asia Times*, May 23, 1996.

Bibliography

Asian Development Bank (1989) *Asian Development Outlook 1989*, Manila.

—— (1990) *Asian Development Outlook 1990*, Manila.

[Australia], East Asia Analytic Unit, Department of Foreign Affairs and Trade (1995) *Overseas Chinese Business Networks in Asia*, Canberra.

Bairoch, P. (1989) "European Trade Policy, 1815–1914," in P. Mathias and S. Pollard (eds), *The Industrial Economies: The Development of Economic and Social Policies (Cambridge Economic History of Europe*, vol. VIII), Cambridge, Cambridge University Press.

—— (1993) *Economics and World History: Myths and Paradoxes*, Hemel Hempstead, Herts., Harvester Wheatsheaf.

Bui Tin (1995) *Following Ho Chi Minh: Memoirs of a North Vietnamese Colonel*, London, Hurst.

Greenfield, G. (1997) "Fragmented Visions of Asia's Next Tiger," in M. Berger and D. Borer (eds), *The Coming of the Pacific Century: East Asia After the Cold War*, London, Routledge.

Hiebert, M. (1996) *Chasing the Tigers: A Portrait of the New Vietnam*, New York, Kodansha International.

International Labour Organization (1994) *Viet Nam: Labour and Social Issues in a Transition Economy*, Bangkok.

International Monetary Fund (1994) *Viet Nam* (IMF Economic Reviews, No. 13), Washington, DC.

—— (1996) *Vietnam: Transition to a Market Economy* (Occasional Paper 135), Washington, DC.

Kerkvliet, B. J. T. and Porter, D. J. (eds) (1995) *Vietnam's Rural Transformation*, Boulder, Col., Westview Press.

Kolko, G. (1963) *The Triumph of Conservatism: A Reinterpretation of American History, 1900–1916*, New York, Free Press.

Nguyen Duc Nhuan (ed.) (1987) *Le Viet Nam post-révolutionnaire: population, economie, société, 1975–1985*, Paris, L'Harmattan.

The Pentagon Papers (1971) Senator Gravel Edition, Boston, Mass., Beacon Press, vol. 2.

Porter, G. (1993) *Vietnam: The Politics of Bureaucratic Socialism*, Ithaca, NY, Cornell University Press.

Probert, J. and Young, S. D. (1995) "The Vietnamese Road to Capitalism: Decentralisation, *de facto* Privatisation and the Limits to Piecemeal Reform," *Communist Economies & Economic Transformation*, vol. 7, pp. 507–15.

Stern, L. M. (1985) "The Overseas Chinese in the Socialist Republic of Vietnam, 1979–82," *Asian Survey*, vol. 25, pp. 521–36.

Tao Zhang and Heng-fu Zou (1996) *Fiscal Decentralization, Public Spending, and Economic Growth in China* (Working Paper No. 1608), Washington, DC, World Bank.

Turley, W. S. and Selden, M. (eds) (1993) *Reinventing Vietnamese Socialism*: Doi Moi *in Comparative Perspective*, Boulder, Col., Westview Press.

World Bank (1996) *From Market to Plan: World Development Report 1996*, New York, Oxford University Press.

World Bank, East Asia and Pacific Region (1993) *Viet Nam: Transition to the Market*, Washington, DC, September 1993.

—— (1995a) *Viet Nam: Poverty Assessment and Strategy*, Washington, DC, January 1995.

—— (1995b) *Viet Nam: Economic Report on Industrialization and Industrial Policy*, Washington, DC, October 17, 1995.

Yingyi Qian (1995) "Reforming Corporate Governance and Finance in China," in Masahiko Aoki and Hyung-Ki Kim (eds), *Corporate Governance in Transitional Economies*, Washington, DC, World Bank.

Index